To my loving husband, Gary, whose life and death created the inspiration and story for this book that will hopefully help others on their journeys through grief.

Only a life lived for others is a life worthwhile.

— Albert Einstein

Widowed in a Heartbeat

A JOURNEY OF GRIEF AND SURVIVAL

Sylvia A. Walters Drake

Walters Publishing House

Copyright © 2022 by Sylvia A. Walters Drake

Widowed in a Heartbeat

Library of Congress Control Number: 2021921254

ISBN: 978-1-7362079-1-8 (paperback)

"I chose to read this book as I was widowed in late February 2020. I highly recommend this book to anyone who has been widowed and to friends of widows who would like to know what to say—and what not to say. I cried through much of my reading but am very glad I read it, and I salute the author for the courage to document her journey; I'm not sure I could do the same."
–Helen Edwards, widow

"I have read this book several times during my seemingly circuitous process (journey) of sorting out a loss of a profound healthy and loving relationship. Reading it during the various phases I felt I was going through was very helpful. Thank you for not making this a how-to book, but rather for impressing upon the reader that this is an individual journey and that 'personal peace needs to be the goal' to understand this lifelong journey."
–Barry Johnson, widower

"I am a widow whose husband died 22 days after Sylvia's. This heartfelt description Sylvia gives of the last few years lets us widows know we are not alone in our grief and struggles. Sylvia's honest and straightforward writing is a blessing for widows as we find ourselves on a journey different from what we envisioned."
–Pat Phillips, widow

"*Widowed in a Heartbeat* clearly relates to any person who is suffering the loss of a spouse, sudden or expected. After I tragically lost my husband of 46 years…I walked this path in a fog of 'grief paralysis' and made decisions based on emotions rather than good judgment. But Sylvia lays out a clear process to bring back purpose and move forward to rebuild a life that is meaningful while holding on to the loving memories of a treasured life." **–Mary Snider, widow**

"This was a great heartfelt story of love and loss and how to handle such a loss. I read this to relate to my mom as this is year five after my father's passing. I will certainly recommend this to her as I know she is still going through stages of grief. This book is helpful for those that lose someone as well as those that want to help others through the loss."

–Amanda P. Klinger, daughter of a widow

"A highlight for grievers reading this book is the *Tomorrow Plan* that can be used as a guide. And something that's applicable to all of us is the tips on what to say and do to a grieving friend or family member. I don't think any of us are without a friend who is grieving right now...or maybe you are the griever. Whichever category you are in, this is a MUST-READ!"

–Debbie Diggs Phillips, friend of the widowed

"This book is much like reading the diary of a close friend. For everyone who has said 'I wish I had realized' or simply didn't know what to say or do, Drake's unabashed honesty can serve as a guide. Through journaling and reflection, she divulges her emotional pain and the struggle to find her footing and shape a new life for herself in the face of her most devastating loss. Highly recommend to those experiencing loss and or supporting someone through the grief journey."   **–Thelma Branson, friend of the widowed**

"Many of the specific feelings described in this book are valid for persons suffering loss of a loved one other than a spouse. The book has helped me focus on my feelings after losing a 32-year-old son. Highly recommend this book for all."   **–Stephen Hepburn, father who lost his son**

CONTENTS

Free Gift

To Help You on Your Journey...

Download your FREE copy of the Tomorrow Plan to help you begin making small changes tomorrow by starting a little plan today.

Don't wait another moment to get started on creating more direction and purpose as you move along from just surviving toward brighter days ahead.

Get your free downloadable **Tomorrow Plan** here:
www.widowedinaheartbeat.com

INTRODUCTION

THE DEATH OF YOUR SIGNIFICANT OTHER IS LIKE
LIVING IN HELL. I KNOW BECAUSE MY HUSBAND
DROPPED DEAD BESIDE ME, LEAVING ME WIDOWED
IN A HEARTBEAT.

I lost the love of my life after thirty-three years of marriage. That dreadful day, I also lost my mind, my heart, my purpose ... my life.

This book is for the widowed (and those who love them). Those who are supporting the widowed will also gain insight into widowhood, which will help them better support their loved ones.

The widowed will relate to this book if they were in a loving relationship with their soulmate, true love, and number one partner. It is not for those who were in a bad or abusive relationship or who felt untouched by the loss of their spouse or partner.

This book describes my journey—the good, the bad, and the ugly. It details the joy of my life, the shattering of my world, the changes I've endured, and the new path I'm navigating. I'm offering insights on my current transition into a life that is a re-creation of me to my very core.

You will witness the full spectrum of the widowed experience from my happy life with my husband to the loss and the devastation. I floundered in an ocean of grief and then began the slow trek to revive the essence of my life.

I am sharing with you the thinking that drove me through grief. Even though it doesn't feel like it, I know now that the rebuilding of my life began the day my world shattered. All the ups and downs, mostly downs at first, all had a place in the rebuilding. It took surviving the grief to start to see the light again.

Grief changes with time. It never fully goes away; it just changes. Deep grief is not a place that you can stay for long. Some say grief is the price you pay for being in love. I guess that just underscores the value of love and how much we should cherish it.

In the first year of being widowed, I tried everything that I could get my hands on to help me through this grief thing. I sought out videos, articles, speakers, research, counselors, and books (especially books) to find shortcuts, expectations, explanations, and answers. The most important answers to me were the how and why of my grief. It was all in search of personal closure.

As I have learned, you too have the power and ability to survive, revive, and thrive after the devastating loss of your spouse. You handle it by dealing with things one at a time and taking baby steps to move along in the experience of being widowed.

By sharing the raw reality of my story, I want you to know that you are not alone in this journey. You can move along and expect better days ahead.

1
WIDOWED

LIFE WAS GREAT.
BUT IN A HEARTBEAT, MY LIFE CHANGED FOREVER.

I have joined A club that I didn't want to belong to. I am a widow. I resent being a part of this club because it has changed my life forever. But here I am. My husband, Gary, unexpectedly dropped dead beside me on February 3, 2017. Life has been a struggle since.

This is a story of intense love, sudden loss, deep grief, and a changed life.

While this story is my reality, memories, and perceptions, the themes are universal. The many experiences and challenges of being widowed are all different yet the same. The things that I say are also sometimes representative of others' experiences, and sometimes not. The main thing we know for sure, for all of us, is that this road is fraught with challenges and changes.

If you're widowed, know that you are not alone and there are others who understand. I have written many things as I lived them, and part of this is just a travel journal of my experiences as well as my reactions along the way. It is sprinkled with memories and the occasionally confusing thoughts about the future. Often my emotions are raw and unfiltered.

This is my life in my first years being widowed. It is the story of how I am moving along with my grief. This journey includes deep sadness along the road of change that I never asked for, never agreed to accept, and have not yet fully comprehended. It is the aftermath of my suddenly being widowed in a heartbeat.

I don't know the outcome of my grief journey and life rebuilding, but I do understand the value of patience and tackling the tough things. I surely must be evolving in ways that are readily apparent, and in other ways that I will only recognize in the future.

There is fear in loss. At least, there was for me. It is not just the loss of the relationship but loss of the very way of life that I once had. Life post-loss forever changes the way we view things.

I have found that I am living two lives. First there is my life, and second is the life of us as a couple. After Gary's death, I was asked what I was going to do. "I'm going to stick to the plan," I snapped. In fact, I did continue with the plans we had as well as what I thought our plans might have been. There was some comfort in not changing any more than I had to.

Regarding survival, one thing that got me from moment to moment was just having something to look forward to. It could be something as simple as planning to talk with a friend on the phone the next day, going to buy a pumpkin spiced latte from my favorite coffee shop, or planning a half-day getaway.

Every aspect of my life changed. Some of it was external—in the way people looked at me and talked to me. But most of it came from within. It was the gut-wrenching reality that only I could address.

Self-talk was a big factor in how I was doing at any point. And what I said to myself changed throughout the years.

Sometimes what you say to yourself is a reflection of what you are thinking. Other times what you say to yourself you will come to believe. Either way, things were tough when I felt sad and negative, and things were better when I was happy and positive. Both my feelings and my self-talk have changed. I found that I needed to tell myself good things in order to start to feel better (even if I didn't believe them at the time).

What I do know is that every year some things have changed, and I will share how some of those things have opened new ways of thinking and doing as I move along the path of life.

First, I want to apologize to everyone in my current situation who I have ever offended unintentionally because I said the wrong thing, talked too much, or did not respond when I should have. I meant to hurt no one; I either thought that I was doing and saying the right things, or I was unsure about what to do or say.

It is impossible for anyone to know how to respond to another's loss, especially death, unless they have experienced the exact same thing. Even then, we all have different takes on death and its effects on us. I believe that we all try our best to use our experiences while attempting to relate to people in pain in a time of loss.

Second, the widowed understand that a person cannot relate to the loss of a spouse unless he or she has experienced that particular loss. Period. No, it is not the same as losing your parent or friend. I have lost both my parents, and I took it badly. I have lost grandparents, aunts, uncles, cousins, friends, and coworkers, as we all have, and those were also gut-wrenching experiences. I cannot speak to how it compares to losing a child or sibling because thankfully I haven't had those experiences. And it certainly is not the same as divorce, losing a pet, getting fired from a job, or any of the other many losses that we endure in our lives.

As tough as many of my losses have been, none of them were even in the same universe as losing my husband. There are so many things that change that it is impossible to list them all. However, I will address some of them here, one at a time, as I saw them.

Third, these writings and assumptions are for those who have had a positive marriage with a spouse or long-term commitment with their soulmate as their best friend. I realize that not all relationships are as good as mine, and that there are other types of reactions to the loss of a spouse. My examples are simply my experiences in the loss of my spouse, best friend, and soulmate, Gary.

Honesty is paramount for me. I feel that I have been at the deepest depths of despair, but there was a ray of hope. It prompted me to start believing in a brighter future. I will share that with you as well.

When dealing with grief, everyone is on their own timeline. I realize that I continued to be consumed with my loss longer than some, and I was able to move along a bit faster than others. There is not a right or wrong way to grieve. It is your grief to do your way.

Sometimes grief seems totally out of your control. Sometimes it feels like you can have an effect on how things are going. And sometimes you feel you are doing better for a while only to backslide. It's not a stead y or predictable journey.

That said, I hope that you will find some comfort in this book as you realize that you are not alone. There are many others of us who relate to your loss, and we are all moving along in our journeys after being widowed in a heartbeat.

2
SOARING–OUR LIFE

WE ENJOYED A LIFETIME OF HAPPINESS
FROM THE MOMENT WE MET.

FALLING IN LOVE – THE FIRST SIX WEEKS

I have always believed in love at first sight. So did Gary. It became a reality when we met.

I was attending a meeting in Kansas City, Missouri, as a representative of the National Agricultural Chemicals Association from Washington, DC. Unlike other boring meetings, the meeting hosts fed us breakfast, lunch, and dinner, held meetings, and threw cocktail parties for all attendees. The first evening of the meeting was Thursday, November 11, 1982—Veterans Day. I was almost late for dinner, so I rushed in the door and sat at the first table available. There happened to be a handsome man sitting beside me. His warm smile and dancing blue eyes caught my attention. It was his wink that melted my heart. That was the first time I met Gary Drake.

As dinner was ending, all of a sudden a very attractive woman came and whispered in Gary's ear and he took off. I thought, *Well, that's that.* I found out the next day that she worked for him. Turns out that her boyfriend, who also worked for him, had hurt his ankle and had to go to the hospital. So it was a very selfless reason for him to abruptly leave.

He sought me out the next day to explain and apologize for his unseemly departure. That evening we attended the cocktail party together. By Saturday night, we were enjoying drinks at the hotel's rooftop restaurant. We'd formed some sort of bond in the two days since we'd met.

As he was talking, I thought to myself, *If he asks me to marry him, I will.*

The next day we both went back to our homes. I flew to Annandale, Virginia, and he drove to Watertown, South Dakota.

For three weeks we spoke on the phone daily for two to four hours. Now that was at the time when you had to pay long distance rates by the minute. We ended up spending $300 to $500 a month just on our calls.

I was scheduled to make a speech in Las Vegas, Nevada, three weeks after we met. Luckily, I was able to divert my flight though Minneapolis, Minnesota. Gary drove to the airport to meet me for our first official date. My heart was in the clouds. As I rushed from the plane into his arms, I was giddy with excitement like a schoolgirl in love for the first time.

He picked me up at 7 p.m. for our first date. By 10 p.m., we had decided that we would get married. We didn't know each other very well, but we knew that we were in love. So we talked for the rest of the weekend about plans to make it happen.

And we spent the following three weeks building our relationship over the phone.

Six weeks after meeting, Gary arrived at my home in Annandale, Virginia, on December 22 with a diamond and traditional proposal on one knee. I accepted. The next day we attended my office Christmas party, and I announced that we were getting married. Needless to say, my boss and everyone there was shocked because they didn't even know I had a boyfriend. We'd just sort of jumped straight into the fiancé-fiancée roles.

One of my coworkers said, "You shouldn't marry someone when you don't even know how they take their coffee."

I said, "We will have plenty of time to find out after we get married."

My boss also asked some awkward questions that were probably illegal then and now. He wanted to know if I was planning to leave my job and follow my husband after I got married.

I said, "No, he is coming to be with me, and I am staying."

He asked when we were getting married, and I told him, "Not until June." That was six months away.

"Oh good," he snapped, "that will give you time to change your mind."

I retorted, "I will not be changing my mind."

PLANNING A WEDDING – THE NEXT FIVE MONTHS

Gary wanted to spend Christmas with me at my parents' home in North Carolina. My parents had never heard of Gary before, but my mother said, "Okay, if that is the only way you'll come home."

On December 24, Gary and I drove to my parents' North Carolina home. We arrived at about 9 p.m. I had a diamond on my hand, and I was nervously turning it since my family and I really didn't yet know this person.

My dad, Gary, and I chatted and drank bourbon for an hour and a half. Things were going pretty well, and I thought they knew him well enough by then. I blurted out that we were getting married.

My mother was in shock, and my father nodded his head and smiled knowingly, as if it all made sense. While opening gifts the next morning, we announced it to my brother and his family.

The next five months involved planning the wedding and Gary's move to Virginia. We met once a month in various states depending on which of us was traveling where. And I made a point of going to South Dakota to meet his family.

We got married on June 11, 1983—exactly seven months after the day we met. It was a very nice wedding, the kind of traditional wedding that I'd always wanted. I was thirty-two years old at the time, and he was thirty-nine. We were at the beginning of a new life together.

Gary moved to Virginia near my Washington, DC job, and he eventually found a job in the area. We spent two honeymoon years there. However, we liked more rural settings. His former employer in South Dakota offered him a job, which we gladly accepted after we had been in one too many DC traffic jams. We enjoyed seven interesting years living in South Dakota. It was comfortable and the right move at the time.

LIVING OUR LIFE – YEARS TWO TO THIRTY-THREE

During those seven years in South Dakota, Gary and I enjoyed getting to know each other and trying to start our family. Eventually we adopted. In 1991, we traveled to Peru and adopted one-month-old Michael. In 1993, we all traveled to Paraguay to get Michael's sister, four-month-old Marisa. Our family was complete.

Both Gary and I were united in our decision to put family first and to do everything that we could to make everything work well for our family of four.

Gary was the best daddy ever. He was kind and thoughtful, devoted and supportive, loving and caring. He spoke in soft tones and never yelled or carried on as I had witnessed some dads do. There were so many precious memories.

When Michael and Marisa were preschoolers, Gary would have "campouts" with Marisa. That meant that they would fall asleep in the living room and stay there all night. And even when she was sound asleep and he could have gone to his own bed without her knowing the difference, he slept there all night. And when Gary was shaving, Michael would smear shaving cream all over his own face and "shave" with his daddy.

We lived in an old farmhouse and fixing it up to our standards has been, of course, a lifelong project. Often when Gary and I were painting, the kids would want to help. My first reaction was to let them stay in the other room and minimize the mess. However, Gary took the time to set them up with their own paint and brushes and papers on the floor. It took more time for setup than actual painting since they were quickly off to other ventures, but he was patient and inclusive.

Gary was Michael's basketball coach, and he was Marisa's avid supporter in her singing, arts, and crafts. When the kids were older, sometimes Gary got them practical things as gifts. One time Michael got tires for his birthday. That made sense. And Marisa got a toilet seat for her bathroom! That was so funny, and the kids and I still chuckle about that.

I adored the ways in which Gary supported the children. And me. They say that the mother is the heart of the home. But I feel that Gary was the heart and soul of our family. I couldn't have asked for anything more.

In between adoptions, we had lived a brief two years in Florida.

We both missed our families, though, so we moved to a small farm in North Carolina to settle and raise Michael and Marisa.

Those years were the most wonderful years of my life. My parents were a quarter mile in one direction, and my brother a quarter mile in the other direction. We enjoyed having my extended family nearby. Of course we also made trips whenever we could to visit his family in South Dakota.

There were dogs, cats, and horses on our North Carolina farm. And we did practically everything as a family, including taking care of our farm. The children were mostly homeschooled, and they enjoyed a rich childhood that included travel, theater, sports, arts, environmental studies, and so much more.

What a great life we had!

PLANNING FOR RETIREMENT

Like so many others, Gary and I lived a very active and interesting life with our children, family, and friends. We worked hard to pursue our careers and make the money we needed to live. And together we invested love, time, and energy into our children, preparing them to be on their own and design their own lives as adults.

After our children had both left for college and jobs around 2015, Gary and I began talking about the future and our time together when we would be alone. We were both ending careers that we had enjoyed, and we were in the process of figuring out exactly how things might work out.

Although we had not completed our retirement plans, the big goal was to just have time together to relax and enjoy just being together. To just feel loved and connected. That was always what we enjoyed most. It didn't matter whether we were going out or staying in. The sweetest times we had together were the ones that were the simplest.

Our Valentine's Day was a quiet evening for us. Gary and I loved to stay home and have a nice meal together, avoiding the crowds. We often chose spots on the far end of the lawn when we attended outdoor concerts so that we could share a few tender moments. We usually were some of the first to leave events, so that we could get home to just relax, chat, and sometimes cuddle together.

We each enjoyed the solitude of being alone in different rooms for a while reading, thinking, and working on projects, only to come back together soon. Just being together had always been our favorite thing. Gary loved laughing at a slapstick comedy movie, and he cherished his time on the phone or in person reminiscing with family and good friends.

For our retirement adventures, Gary and I had planned to purchase a small travel trailer. Our plan was to spend several weeks of our summer traveling cross-country. We had discussed cutting our work hours, and we were going to take the spring to make our retirement plans.

As Gary was waiting to hear about budget cuts at work, he was planning to reduce his hours and head toward retirement. The cuts came February 3, 2017, the morning he died. He never had a chance to present his proposal to the Board of Directors at their meeting the following week.

THOUGHTS ABOUT GARY'S DEATH

Gary's death has impacted everything that I think and feel at this time. Although I will probably change my mind again about some things, here are issues that have been first and foremost in my mind.

Life is too short to let so many things bother us—what we should have done, what we should not have done, what we should have done better, what we should or should not have done with our kids, parents, spouse, friends ... so many hypothetical situations.

Then there is also what we think we need to do—sort through old photos, send a birthday card, mow the lawn, do the dishes, etc. The list of things to worry about seems endless.

But the truth is that none of it matters the way that we think it does.

Every generation thinks they have the answer, and every individual thinks they will save the world. The truth is that for most of us—almost all of us—the only thing we will ever affect is the moment. And our moments can be gone before we know it, and it seems like nobody cares because each person is doing the best he or she can in his or her own moment to get along.

When we die, the world will still have good and evil despite the efforts to enrich the good and because of the continued destruction from the bad.

People will still be aging, getting sick, and dying even though modern medicine will cure some diseases and prolong life for some. Others of lesser means will die sooner and more miserably because they do not have access to modern care.

Money will still be the basis for much good like building hospitals, donating food, and saving animals. Money also will be the root of all evil as people use it as power, destroying the environment and dividing classes of people.

The world will be mostly the same, except that we are gone.

SO WHAT MATTERS?

Moment to moment, being sure that your thoughts and actions were what you wanted them to be. That matters.

Moment to moment, not giving way to worry and regret when you can choose to love and give. That matters.

Moment to moment, making someone else's life better in a way that you feel good about (but not if you feel used or overextended or resentful). That really matters.

I think that's it.

I'm not there yet.

I really just want my husband back.

3
"D" Day–The Death

AFTER LUNCH ON FEBRUARY 3, 2017, MY WORLD
CRASHED.

It started like any normal Friday. Gary followed a very meticulous schedule that efficiently accomplished the most in the least amount of time. He got up, took a shower, brushed his teeth, dried immaculately, and completed all the usual morning rituals. He called me to take my turn in the shower as he dressed, made the bed, and checked that no clothes were left lying around. Then he went into his home office and read his devotional.

As we were leaving for work, I rushed past him out the door. I remember on the way giving a quick kiss and saying, "Love you. Gotta go. See you later."

He replied, "Okay, I love you." He also said that he just wasn't feeling that great.

I, too, was not feeling that great, and we were both looking forward to a relaxing weekend at home together. He went to work and received an email he was expecting about a cut in funding. When I called him at 10:30 to ask about lunch, he said that he had to get notification emails out and was not sure about lunch and to call him back at noon. I did, and he said he was mostly done and that we could meet at home to decide about lunch since our daughter had stayed home sick with tonsillitis.

When we arrived home, Gary was interested in having lunch in our little town of Welcome, so he offered to bring our daughter some food and we left. He again said he wasn't really feeling good. I offered to drive and get the food, or drive us there, but he said no. We sat and ate without much talking. We were both just plain exhausted.

He said again after lunch that he didn't feel great. I offered to drive us home, but once again, he said no, he would do it.

Gary was totally devoted to his mission as Executive Director of Cancer Services of Davidson County. There was a fundraising event coming up, and we always had signs in our yard promoting these events. As we pulled into the driveway, he asked me to set out a sign. He explained that he didn't feel like getting out of the car. (He always did it himself before.) Before I answered, he said he would do it, but I insisted I would and jumped out of the car with the sign.

After we went in the house, he handed a bag of to-go food to our daughter. I remember saying she needed a plate, so he took it in the kitchen and put it on a plate. Then he went upstairs, changed, and pulled together some laundry. When he came back down, he said he had tripped coming down the stairs. I asked him why he tripped, but he didn't know. I commented that he needed to be careful.

Gary left the laundry basket at the bottom of the stairs, which he had never done, and again he said he felt bad and was going to sit in the other room and look at some papers. He also said that Marisa and I could stay in the living room and watch our "stupid shows" on TV. Marisa and I chuckled at the time. He was not interested in reality shows about wedding dresses or retro shows before the 90s.

I was looking at my computer before going outside to treat

our horse's wound. Thank goodness I had not left yet. After about five minutes, I heard him say in a low eerie voice, "Sylvia ... Sylvia, please come here."

I went to him, and he said, "Either something is wrong, or I am having anxiety over feeling bad. My pulse is racing."

I got the cuff and took his blood pressure, which was normal. But his pulse was 176. I thought surely that was wrong and took it again and it measured 178. I said, "Do you want me to call 911?"

He said no.

"Do you want me to take you to the hospital?"

He said no.

"Do you want me to call the doctor?"

"Yes, okay."

I said that I was going to call the rheumatoid arthritis doctor since he had been concerned about some meds that he had taken for the second time that morning. He said no, that was the wrong person.

I told him I did not know the regular doctor's number. In my panic, I was blanking. He said get his book and he pointed to a number. He pointed to the wrong number, which was unlike him, and I called the correct number to be told that it was Friday afternoon, and the doctors were gone.

As I was asking what I should do, I heard his papers hit the floor and he gasped. I turned to hand him his papers as I saw his head jerk from left to right, then drop on his chest before he went totally limp.

I looked at him, sat beside him, and kissed him, but there was no response. I thought I needed to start CPR and looked at him again. All the while I was saying *I love you* and *stay with me*. I refused to say come back because I didn't want him to think that I thought he was dying. But I already knew that he was gone.

I said to Gary (and myself), "No, you're not dying." And I screamed his name. I lifted his head and it dropped. I tilted his head, put my lips on his and tried to blow life back into him. As I yelled for my daughter to call 911, she had already done so when she heard the first scream. They had her put me on speaker phone and barked orders for getting him on the floor to begin CPR. I pulled gently, but he didn't budge.

I yelled for Marisa to help me, and we jerked him out of the recliner. His head popped on the floor, and I knew it hurt his bulging disc. I remember feeling bad about that, but I think I told myself we would just fix it later. *Why didn't I say it out loud so he could hear me?*

I saw his eye slowly roll toward me. I thought it might be involuntary, but if it were deliberate, he was using all his strength. I don't know for how long he could hear my screams and I love yous.

The 911 operator was directing me to do compressions. (I had learned CPR way back in college but not used it since.) I knew I wasn't doing it hard enough, Marisa said I was doing it wrong, so she did a few. I was exhausted. All the operator could say was that I wasn't doing it hard enough. They said listen and push. I kept yelling, "I need help. When is someone going to get here?"

She said they are on the way and to do what she said till they arrived.

I kept going as best I could, which was not good enough. Six minutes after the 911 call, a paramedic flew into the house and shouted, "Move, I'm taking over." He asked how long this had been going on.

I frantically cried out, "Fifteen minutes, maybe twenty. Where have you been?"

The truth was that it was only six minutes from the time of the 911 call till they arrived. The longest six minutes of my life.

In just moments, it seemed there were about six more people in the room, and they could not get a response. I kept saying to Gary before and after they came, "The right people are on the way to help you," and "I love you." I said that over and over. They told me to keep talking to him.

While they were working on him, they tried everything possible. They did CPR, three shock treatments, and meds to get a faint pulse going. They wanted a pulse before leaving for the hospital. Originally they said they were taking him to the closest hospital, but I wanted him to go to the heart specialists. They left for the hospital, and I nervously drove by myself.

My daughter wanted to stay home, so my brother stayed with her. In the meantime, she had called the key people in our lives—the main people who needed to know. While I was on the road, I called my son to update him about what was happening. I projected that there was a fifty-fifty chance that his dad would die.

In my mind, I was thinking it's more than 95% chance that he wouldn't make it. I told my son that it wouldn't surprise me if they were waiting for me at the door to tell me he had not even made it to the hospital. And yes, when I went in, they met me and took me to a private room. That's always a bad sign.

The doctor said, "You have to let him go."

I asked what was going on.

She said, "We're doing CPR, but it's been too long, and he's not had oxygen to his brain in about an hour and a half from the beginning of the episode until now."

I knew that was true, but I demanded more. "I want to see him."

She said, "No, you need to let him go."

But she didn't know me. She didn't know us. I insisted on seeing him.

When I burst into the room, one of the medics was jumping

on him trying to get him going, and several others were standing around watching. I looked for a moment and then I said calmly, "I'm told that I should let him go. Is that what I need to do?" And I looked at every single person's face; none of them made a move since they are not allowed to give any indication of anything.

So I said, "I'll take that as a yes. Let him go."

They asked me two more times, forcing me to confirm it. "Yes, let him go."

After they stopped, I mumbled, "I guess that was the right thing to do." Out of the corner of my eye, I detected several heads nodding slightly.

Then I told them to take all the tubes and wires off him and leave me alone with him. I think that's what they do anyway.

As soon as they had everything removed, I went in to spend one final time alone with my heartthrob. He was gone. I had one last opportunity to hold his hand, touch his body, tell him *I love you*, and hug him. I laid my head in the cradle of his right shoulder, my favorite place where he had always provided comfort and love. I repeatedly whispered *I love you* as if pleading with him to say it back. *Always and forever*. I sat quietly beside him. I just spent time with him.

I had to call my daughter and son and let them know that yes, he definitely was gone. It was the hardest day of my life. I stayed with his cooling body until his coworker and the funeral home showed up.

Then the post-death activities began. Little did I know what was in store for the rest of my life.

Marisa had stayed home to straighten up and move the furniture back. She thought that I wouldn't want to come back to that. I called Gary's sister and two other relatives and asked them to let everyone else know.

Our cousin had lost her husband in the same way a few years earlier. Her first comment was, "Oh no! I didn't want anyone else to have to go through that."

That comment was my instant realization of the future sadness that would continue to unfold. In fact, all widows have said less to me than other people who were not widowed. Having experienced it, they knew that this moment was the tip of the iceberg.

That day was the end of our worldliness together and the beginning of the rest of my life alone. All I knew was that I wanted my husband back.

I will love Gary, always and forever.

4
THE FIRST FEW DAYS –
WHAT'S HAPPENING?

MY NEW LIFE BEGAN WITH A FLURRY OF EVENTS
AND EMOTIONS.

THE BEGINNING OF THE END

Just twenty-one months before Gary died, we had a full house. We had two dogs, two cats, two horses, two children in and out between college and jobs, and the two of us.

First, our little Maltese dog, Annabell, died from COPD and broke our hearts. At the time, our son had moved to Florida, and our daughter was moving to college. Some months later, my favorite cat, Gray, was on the outside windowsill and disappeared that night. I know that a coyote got the cat since Gray liked to go out after dusk and play around the barns.

Then one of our horses, Scout, was acting very strange. Gary happened to be home one day when he noticed and told me to go on to work while he kept an eye on him. That evening just before my night class, Gary called to update me on Scout, "He was running and acting frantic. No, now he is eating hay and fine now … he just fell over … he's dead!" I was later told it was most likely an aneurism or heart attack.

Four months after Scout died, Gary dropped dead beside me. It seemed the loss of our pets was the beginning of the end.

Suddenly, the house was much emptier. My daughter, who had been home for a few months, moved back to Boone in the mountains as planned. My son was already back in Orlando. Everyone had left to go back to where they live. And I was alone.

There was now one horse, one dog, one cat, and one person. We had all lost our mates. For all of us life would never be the same.

SHORT-TERM FAMILY PLAN

The second day after Gary's death, we had a family meeting—me with my two young adult children, Michael, twenty-five, and Marisa, twenty-three. I said that there were three things that we as a family would do.

First, we would all be nice to each other no matter what our feelings were.

Second, we would do whatever it took to get through the funeral in North Carolina and the memorial visitation in South Dakota.

Third, we would go back to doing whatever we were doing before he died after the two weeks that we were all taking off.

I did not want my children to feel that they needed to change their lives for me. I didn't really know all the changes that were ahead of me either. At the time, Michael lived ten hours away in Orlando, and Marisa was planning to move in a few months back to Boone, North Carolina, two hours away. They each had jobs, significant others, and their own lives.

As for me, I decided to follow much of the plan that my husband and I had laid out. There were places to go, things to do, and ideas to pursue on our 2017 agenda. Although we had planned more discussions in the next few weeks, I at least knew (or thought I knew) most of it. Having done the paperwork for the death of my mom and dad, I already knew that the paperwork and logistics would consume me for several months.

FUNERAL AND MEMORIAL SERVICE

My husband had been the CEO of Hospice of Davidson County for fifteen years. He retired from there for three years and then took a position as Executive Director of the fledgling Cancer Services of Davidson County. He had been at that job five years when he died. He was well known in our area's nonprofit community.

Gary died on a Friday—too late for anything to be put in the paper on Saturday morning, and there was no local paper on Sunday and Monday. When I went to the funeral home and requested that we do the service on Tuesday, I was told that couldn't happen. The phone had been ringing off the hook at the funeral home, and people wanted to know what was going on; we had to wait until Wednesday to give people a chance to find out and be there.

I didn't have to submit the obituary until Monday night, and it took me the entire three days to write it. I just couldn't concentrate. I was in shock. I was devastated. My mind was blank. I felt helpless. All these feelings engulfed me more every time I tried to write anything. Grief muddles things, and it's difficult to summarize the brilliance of a life when you haven't fully processed that the life is gone. Fortunately for me, I was able to put my hands on his most recent bio for guidance.

I was surprised by the explosive communications about his death. The night he died, everyone knew! People were all trying to figure out what happened. Countless people did the only thing that they knew to do or say, which was to bring food. In fact, so much food was brought the day after Gary passed away that friends were calling others and asking them to not bring any more food. And there I was with a house of overflowing food, still trying to comprehend my loss.

There were friends who wanted to help, and I asked them to get the food packaged and refrigerated. I decided that much of it would be used for the meal to be served after the funeral for family.

For five hours on Tuesday night, we stood at the funeral home in the never-ending line of people as more kept pouring in. I know some people had come at other times during the day and signed the book. And even more came and didn't sign the book, as the funeral director later told me.

On Wednesday, we had the funeral that I had meticulously planned (at least as best I could) to make it as meaningful as possible. I think the service was all he would have wanted it to be. Because we had never discussed services and how to proceed with such arrangements, I was making it all up as I went.

I also met with my two children to tell them what I was thinking about the funeral, so I could include their input and wishes. They approved the obituary, funeral plans, and everything else. But mostly they were interested in just supporting whatever I thought I wanted. They both participated in the funeral, my son by making comments about his dad and my daughter by singing a solo. I was too upset and stunned to participate in any other way than just sitting there.

We rushed home after the funeral service to find one more dear friend waiting there; she wanted to visit for a short while. After she left, I told my children they had one hour to pack their bags for us to drive 1,200 miles from our home in Welcome, North Carolina, to Watertown, South Dakota, Gary's hometown. We were having a memorial visitation for family and friends there.

We left at about 8 p.m. in the snow and drove two hours. After a night in the hotel, we found the snow had let up the next morning. The kids and I drove instead of flying because the memorial visitation would have all the pictures and artifacts that had been at the visitation in North Carolina.

We spent the entire day Thursday driving while we were on the phone, lining things up for the visitation. Gary's relatives had rented a hall and decided that a memorial visitation, a come-and-go-as-you-please event, would be perfect for Saturday afternoon. And it was just the right thing.

I had additional activities in mind to honor the memory of my husband. His love was bigger than just the love for me and Michael and Marisa—it extended to family and friends. And it extended to strangers whose good and welfare concerned him deeply.

I sent a picture of the roses by his casket to a florist in Watertown, South Dakota. I asked that she re-create that particular design in carnations. You see, Valentine's Day was coming up, and it was a very special time for Gary. He always bought a lot of carnations and even made fudge to give to family, coworkers, and friends. It was something he was known for.

I had wanted carnations at the funeral, but it was hard to get them because of all of the Valentine's Day celebrations. The carnations that were placed in the floral arrangements for the memorial visitation had a dual purpose. I had called hospice in Watertown and asked that those carnations be delivered after the service to all hospice patients on Valentine's Day. It was a gesture made in Gary's memory. I wanted them to know that their hometown boy had been a driving force in a hospice in another state. So that is what we did. It was a nice touch and a good use of the flowers in a way that Gary would have appreciated.

MORE DEATHS

Gary had friends who were very near and dear to him. When we visited South Dakota the summer before he passed away, he made a point of visiting his two friends, Ernie and Bonnie. We had kept up with them through cards and visits throughout the years.

Ernie had been sick for the year prior and died in December 2016, just before Gary.

After that death, we learned that Bonnie had cancer and was in hospice. She had been talking to Gary regularly for a month or so before his death. When I went to see her before the memorial visitation, she explained that he had been counseling her. He had never stated it that way. He always just told me he had nice talks with Bonnie. Two weeks after the memorial service, Bonnie also died.

Another friend who he kept up with regularly was Bob from Texas. After Gary died, Bob and I spoke a few times about Gary and how shocked we both were about Gary's sudden death. Bob told me that he had had heart problems but had been managing them for several years. When he was in the hospital a few months later, I texted and he texted me back. The next day he died too.

Four friends died within five months. I remember hoping so deeply that perhaps I could have a year without a death on my property or near me.

DIFFICULTIES WITH GARY'S DEATH

There were three things that made Gary's death extremely difficult for me.

First, Gary was my spouse. He was my lover, my confidant, my true love, my one and only, the man of my dreams, the person I intended to spend the rest of my life with. This was a relationship like no other that I had ever had, or intended to ever have again.

Second, this was the first time that I had lost someone who I was living with at the time. That's very different. It means that you can never have the chance to be in a place that gives you a few moments of relief from their absence.

Third, it was so sudden. I was literally widowed in a heartbeat. I was beyond shocked. All deaths are difficult. Yet sometimes you know that something is coming and perhaps some grieving occurs in advance. I don't know. But the sudden shock turned into a pounding grief drenching my body and soul like a relentless rainstorm.

MY NEW LIFE

Gary's death represented the end of my life as I knew it. The sheer bliss of having a happy marriage and tight-knit, loving family instantly shattered my present-day heart and crushed my dreams for the future. The dreams I had of retiring and slipping into the sunset with my true love by my side transformed into an unbearable nightmare.

5
YEAR ONE OF DOING THE GRIEF – THE LITTLE THINGS

YEAR ONE CAUSED FAR MORE CHANGES
THAN I COULD HAVE IMAGINED.

THERE ARE NO SHORTCUTS

DURING THE FIRST few years, there were times that I wanted to move fast, jump ahead, abandon grief, and forget the past. But I couldn't. My heart and soul would not let me. There are no shortcuts to "doing" the grief.

Some people move through the worst of it quicker than others. The truth is that the length, breadth, and depth of your grief is not an indicator of the love, commitment, and quality of your relationship. There is no prescribed length of time, breadth of activities, or depth of despair that defines grief. Grief is different for everyone.

Although many elements are the same, grief is truly individualized.

The experience was so new to me in this way that I wondered if I was losing my mind completely. Now I know that, yes, maybe I was losing my mind, but it was normal under the circumstances.

Some people have grieved in advance of a death, like when someone is terminally ill. (I know this was true for me when my mother was slowly dying for several years from Alzheimer's.)

I believe that everyone has a personal Grief Factor. You'll put in that amount of grief—no more, no less. Whatever grieving you do is based on your Grief Factor.

It was normal to not know what to do even though I was not clear about that at the time. It was normal for others as well as myself to be surprised at how I responded to anything and everything. It was normal to be confused. It was normal to cry for no reason. It was normal to, well, be all the crazy things that I was.

Some of my friends thought maybe I was losing it, so I was reluctant to be totally honest with them. But really I was just surviving in a new (ab)normal that was common to many who had lost a beloved spouse.

Sometimes people have shorter or longer time frames for dealing with grief than I did. That's another aspect of the Grief Factor. Some people would not handle things as I chose to.

I know that the road we each take is not an indicator of who loved whom more or less. It is just the difference in us all. So however your Grief Factor will manifest, it is probably right for you.

GRIEVING IS EXHAUSTING

If I thought I had tired days before Gary died, the grieving process accelerated exhaustion to a whole new level. I stayed depleted and generally lacked the energy—and the heart—to get many things done.

A counselor had told me that grieving is healing, and healing requires energy. Wow, was that right! All of the changes and challenges surrounding loss and grief demand more energy than one could ever imagine.

That is partly what is meant when the widowed are encouraged to take baby steps. Navigating uncharted territory and mustering the energy to do so are slowed down by your grief-induced depletion of energy.

EVERYTHING IS AFFECTED

Gary's death affected everything. There is nothing in my life that remains the same.

If you have not been widowed, you cannot fully understand this concept. When two people live together, and are soulmates and best friends, their lives becomes intertwined in ways that they don't even recognize until the other is gone.

That's what happened to me. There are, of course, the big decisions that were impacted. But the small decisions have been just as difficult and frustrating too. I'll share a few of those seemingly small things here.

The coffee pot. I cannot tell you the number of times I had to turn around and drive back home when I was halfway to work. Gary and I both thought that it was very important to turn off the coffee pot every morning and prevent a potential fire hazard. We did it every day. I probably did it half the time, and he did it the other half. But he always checked it before he left. He was the last line of defense for coffee-pot-turning-off. Because we had this joint responsibility, sometimes I simply had no recollection if I had done it before heading out the door.

Got milk? After Gary died, there was never any milk in the house. Gary had always picked up milk on the way home. It wasn't that I didn't want to have milk. I did. But I could never remember to pick it up even though I was in grocery stores many days. I just couldn't seem to make that change to remember to get it myself.

Food. Eating and mealtimes became an issue for me. When we were together, we would make a decision about what to eat and whether to go out or stay home.

For example, I used to call Gary just to find out what we would be doing for supper. I would make the call, we would have a short conversation, and we would hang up. I would go back to my work and he would go back to his.

But once he was gone, when it was the time that I usually called, there was no one to call. It upset me. It was sad.

Now I must always decide what to eat. Some days I just don't want to make those decisions, so I just eat peanut butter crackers for a meal. I didn't realize how much of a social event it was for my husband and me to eat anything, anywhere, anytime. But now I recognize what a team effort food was every day.

Dump Day. This may seem odd, but we had a reprieve from life with our Dump Day chores. And now it will never be the same. Gary and I always took the trash to the dump every two weeks. We waited until we could both go. This had been ongoing for years. Although we were gone less than thirty minutes, I considered it to be quality talk time for just us. We were by ourselves, like on a date, especially if everything else had been family oriented that week.

When Gary died, the dump run changed. No longer was it something I looked forward to. It became another chore. And driving alone reminded me that he wasn't here. After some weeks, I started taking my Golden Retriever, Sandie, with me. Now she has become my dump date. Not the same, but a worthy second choice.

Washing dishes. I always needed to do dishes. It seemed like an overwhelming task to take them off the counter and out of the sink and put them in dishwasher even though I passed them many times each day. As I was sitting one evening (unable to move), I finally came up with a plan. I would put one dish in the dishwasher each time I passed it. It took several times passing it before I actually did it. After I put one in, the next time I put in two, and so on. Eventually it was full, and I could turn the dishwasher on. Over the course of a few months, I continued the exercise until I was back to normally completing this daily task.

The fridge filter. Then there was the pesky filter for our fridge water. I have always known that it gets changed every few months. But Gary always took care of that. When the red light indicated time to change the filter, I did know to take the old one with me and ensure that I purchased the correct type. I managed to put it back in. However, when I threw the old one away, I didn't take off the handle for pulling the next one out. It took months before I realized what I had done. I had to order another handle.

That's what my fellow widows meant by baby steps. Doing the least little thing is a big victory.

I continued this pattern with other small things. I couldn't just clean the room. I would try to dust one day (or even just dust one thing a day), vacuum another day, put papers away another day. And even that would take a week for one room. After months, the time frame shortened for getting things done.

My life is affected at every level by the loss of my husband, and the list is seemingly endless.

But mostly, I feel alone.

LOSING IT

I would cry for any or no reason.

I would feel deep depression envelop me at odd times.

I would suddenly scream and cry out, "I just want my husband back!" And I did it as many times as I could muster, often accompanied by sobbing.

One night, I really did lose it. I ran around the house screaming and yelling, "I just want my husband back." My Golden Retriever went nuts. She had never witnessed anything like this. Then I plopped down at the kitchen table and wrote furiously almost 200 times, "I just want my husband back," chanting wildly as I scribbled. After about thirty minutes, I stopped everything.

I was exhausted.

These types of random behaviors became a normal part of my life during the first year.

WIDOW'S FOG

I had heard of Widow's Fog (sometimes called Widow Brain and other variations). But I never knew what it was till I experienced it.

It means just what it implies—being in a fog because you are now widowed. The fog obscures our judgment, impairs our sight, makes us feel sluggish, and just generally eliminates clarity of mind, body, soul, and spirit. Cognitive thinking is difficult and sometimes close to impossible.

My understanding is that Widow's Fog is a universal reaction, not just the reaction within a certain culture, country, religion, or any other single group. Indeed, I understand it happening. Being at a loss for dealing with as massive of a change as widowhood is a very real thing, especially when it's someone you've loved so deeply.

For me, nothing was clear. I felt like I was in a constant fog. I could not think or see clearly. Sometimes I could not think beyond the moment. Sometimes, in a moment of clarity, the fog set in like the thick fogs that blanket the coast some mornings. Everything became unclear, unsure, and unsettled in an instant.

Then there were the daily living challenges. Never had I had so many times that I forgot a name I knew or couldn't find what I was looking for (only to find it in the first place I looked where it should have been). I often couldn't answer easy questions and definitely couldn't make the simplest of decisions. This was **every day**.

And as fog does, it comes and goes at random times, even years after Gary's death.

DON'T CONFUSE DOING SOMETHING WITH DOING WELL

People were constantly observing what I was doing from the moment that they found out that Gary died. They were paying attention to whether I was taking it well or taking it badly. They especially noticed whether I was doing things or not doing things.

This constant observation was difficult many times. Actually, it was difficult all the time. I continued to work my job. I also completed all the post-death tasks of changing names, paying bills, stopping payments, reporting change of status, etc.

I was the sole caretaker for my house and property. Several times I bit off more than I could chew and got myself in a bind. Thankfully I had friends and family who helped me muddle through those times. It was critical that I readjusted my thinking to be clear on what one person, not two, could realistically do.

Yes, I did do some traveling and other things. These were interesting activities. It was very discouraging when people came up to me and said, "I'm glad to see you're out having fun. I'm glad to see you're doing so well."

Seriously?

Mainly it just meant that I was lonely and having my nightly cry at a different place. But that's a significant part that people don't understand about the experience of losing a spouse.

So don't confuse doing something with doing well. There's the physical act of getting things done and doing what must be done. And then there's the emotional crush of the whole situation. People can be functioning on one level but dying on the other.

ADDING INSULT TO INJURY

One day in the first month after Gary passed away, I had a problem with my vacuum cleaner. I took it to our vacuum cleaner dealer and decided while driving that there was no fixing it. I would just buy a new one. It was an irrational last-minute decision because I hadn't even found out what was wrong with my vacuum. I had heard about widows spending money without thinking it through, and I was determined to not be that widow.

Yet when I got to the store, I explained that I had a broken vacuum cleaner, and I didn't want it anymore. I wanted a new one.

The store clerk proceeded to explain to me that they had a special going that day, and they would check my vacuum for free to see what was wrong, give me a trade-in price on a new one, and let me keep the old one. I even argued with them about why I shouldn't keep my old one! By the way, the repair cost only $25. I didn't need another vacuum. But by then, I had already purchased a new one for $500. Eventually I walked out with two working vacuums.

The worst thing was when they looked up our account and they asked, "Is this the account for Gary Drake?" I fell apart sobbing uncontrollably, much to their surprise.

I said, "Yes, it is his. No, he's not here." And I continued blubbering, confusing the clerk.

In another case, I had to go to the cable company to make some changes to our service. They would not allow me to do anything because the TV service was in his name only. So once again I proceeded to absolutely fall apart in front of the salesperson and other customers.

I found out later that occasionally happens, and I was not the first. I had to go and find paperwork that proved that he had died to even get my name on my service so that I could make a change.

These encounters—being reminded of things that Gary handled—only added insult to injury. Even though I had lived alone before we were married and knew how to get things done, when you're under emotional duress like that, it's hard to think.

There were numerous other situations, too, like when I had to change names on the banking accounts, utilities, and more. Each time it was like he died all over again. And again. And again.

IT'S CONFUSING – I OR WE? MINE OR OURS?

The entire first year, I found that I had problems with pronouns. For over thirty-three years I referred to everything as *we* and *us* and *ours*. Now I found that I needed to be using the words *I* or *me* or *mine*.

All of a sudden when I was asked something about an account, or the house, or work, or whatever, I would be talking about *how we do this* and *we are doing that*. Then in the next sentence, I would be using the word *I did this* and *I do that*. I didn't want to let him go, so I purposefully continued talking about what we did and what we like and how we handle certain situations.

I know the people talking with me noticed that I had a problem with pronouns, and whether I used past or present tense verbs. But making the language transition was a more confusing situation than anyone can ever imagine. As long as I could, I both consciously and subconsciously denied that Gary was gone. And it showed in my language.

I have been asked countless times when I think about my husband the most. From the beginning, I said I thought about him all the time. It felt like going insane, like my mind could never rest.

The only break my mind had was when I was in my classroom teaching. Sure, I had assignments to grade and meetings to attend too. But I did not have a break until I was actively focused on teaching. Gary had told me that he never thought about us when he was in a board meeting and dedicating his focus on the business at hand. So my teaching, which I enjoy, offered the occasional reprieve.

At work, we might call each other at any time, so he was constantly on my mind the rest of the day. And I felt the same way in the car. And at home. And everywhere. So when I wasn't teaching, I was never able to get him off my mind. In fact, I thought I would lose my mind.

To someone who is not widowed, that may not make sense. In fact, one friend told me I couldn't think about him all the time because I wasn't with Gary all the time before. It's a funny thing how absence works. The fact that Gary was not with me was highlighted in so many ways all day long, every day.

He is not there for me to call. He can't answer the door if my hands are wet. He can't call me. He isn't there to discuss the day with me to help put things into perspective. This list is endless. ...

EMBRACE THE BELIEFS THAT COMFORT YOU

What are your beliefs? All of your beliefs, from spirituality and religion, to personal values and humanity. Explore those beliefs and cling to those that give you comfort.
Here are five of the personal beliefs that I have been exploring.

First, my spiritual and religious beliefs. In my case, this was a time in which I have questioned everything I believed or thought I knew. Although I returned to some of my beliefs, I abandoned others. Whatever faith, beliefs, hopes, and dreams give you comfort, by all means embrace them.

People often say everything happens for a reason. But does it really? Maybe. I don't know. I certainly felt before that everything happened for a reason. Now I am thinking that maybe some things just happen, and it is our reaction and our reason for reacting the way we do that is the lesson.

Second, my beliefs about the relationship Gary and I had. Was it as good as I remember? Were the regrets as important as I thought? Was my life really better as a result of this relationship? During this time after death, a time to reflect on everything, there are some things that were perhaps more or less important than I thought at the time.

Of course, we know that hindsight is 20/20. So having this new perspective could be part of my learning experience from our relationship. I am the only person who can see things from this perspective since I am the only one who really knows the breadth and depth of our relationship.

Third, my beliefs about taking my past with me into the present and the future. How could you not? I know that many people talk about leaving the past behind. Are you kidding me?! I have only my past, present, and future. I am not about to leave behind the one-third that made me who I am today.

Of course, you can't live in the past, and you need to concentrate on the present and the future. Nonetheless, your past is your foundation for the present and the future. I intend to enjoy my memories, and now I can pick and choose those that support me in my present and my future.

I don't have to relive the stress of a job or worry about bills or frustration with family and friends. I can and do choose to remember the happy times, the funny stories, the touch of his hand, his wink, the strong arms that lifted me up when I fell. Those are the memories that dominate my thoughts as I go forward. These are the things that give me peace in the moment, satisfaction in where I am now in life, and relief that I did make it through so many tough things.

Fourth, my beliefs about intuition. Intuition is important. I believe in intuition and the ability to just know something without positive proof at that moment. I believe that generally people fare better when they follow their intuition. I am working to make that an even bigger part of my life.

Fifth, my beliefs about my place in the world. As a member of this earth, I feel an obligation to give back in whatever ways I can. This may involve volunteering hours to help homeless pets, donating money to veterans' organizations, and supporting environmental causes. It will involve treating everyone as they should be treated regardless of how different they may be. It can be as simple as opening a door for the person ahead of me or assisting a disoriented stranger.

I hope to be a contributor in the world to support an atmosphere of love and peace. It starts at home and goes with me wherever I go. After all, if I am not a part of the solution, I am part of the problem.

So beliefs are not just about believing. They are about taking action. And I do believe that taking action in anything you care about helps you as well as the people and cause you have selected.

Bottom line—embrace the beliefs that comfort you. And then act on them.

6
AN INTERLUDE FROM MY JOURNAL

WRITING ABOUT MY FEELINGS WAS ENLIGHTENING
AND REVEALING TO ME.

I kept a journal every day during the first year. The main reason was because I had an intense drive to express my feelings and frustrations somewhere. Many of my journal entries were almost completely "I love you," "I miss you," and "I just want my husband back."

I would encourage others to keep a journal and write down thoughts whenever you are feeling lonely, frustrated, analytical, contemplative, or otherwise wishing to address your grief. It can be both comforting at that moment and useful months later in offering you perspective on what has changed or remained the same in your journey.

Following are some of my more insightful entries; they are my raw thoughts from when I was in the midst of grieving.

REFLECTION – THE PAIN OF THE BEST KIND OF LOVE

Friday, April 7, 2017 – Two months after death

It was simple.

It was deep.

It was real.

It was honest.

It was always and forever.

This describes the best kind of love … The love I shared with my husband of 33+ years.

Upon the sudden and unexpected death of my dear husband, Gary, my life changed forever. In the two short months since February 3, 2017 around 3 p.m., I have experienced a new life, one that I did not want.

I have felt the deepest sad imaginable. I have nothing to compare it to. It goes beyond the depths of my heart and seems to go straight through my soul to uncharted territory.

It occasionally touches the dreaded feeling of hopelessness which is paralyzing all by itself. It is a place that I try to avoid because no one can live there for long. It is a place of death. The kind of death that you hope leads to nothingness to make the indescribable sadness go away.

I THINK I KILLED MY HUSBAND
(AND NOW I AM LIVING WITH THE GUILT)

June 14, 2017 – Four months after death

I think I killed my husband.

I didn't mean to. There is the kind of killing that is pre-meditated and intentional. There is the kind of killing that is accidental. Then there is the kind of killing I committed. That is the killing by not doing all that you can within your power to assure that someone lives.

I knew that Gary had something going on, and so did he. We confirmed the beginning of the rheumatoid arthritis, and he had just taken his second pill that day. The diagnosis and prescribed treatment for RA went as it should, and I was with him at doctor appointments too.

However, I did not go with him to his general practitioner the last time, just a few days before he died.

I should have. And I should have insisted that I go back to the room with him.

This doctor's office did not allow that. In fact, I was not allowed to go back to him one time before when I was late arriving at his appointment. If I had been there that day, perhaps I could have added a crucial bit of information to help find the problem.

Gary had not been feeling totally right for months (never missing work or anything like that). But he was tested for all sorts of autoimmune and other diseases including lupus, Rocky Mountain spotted fever, anemia, and had an electrocardiogram and stress tests just weeks before his death. Clearly, he needed something different. All along I had suggested trying some other doctors as well, but he wanted his doctor to complete and exhaust all his options. This doctor was much trusted by Gary, but semi-retired and not quickly available for appointments.

This doctor had told Gary many months before to stop taking baby aspirin since the benefits for the heart were probably outweighed by, I think he said, the possible problems of internal bleeding. That didn't seem to work out well for Gary.

Also, we received a mailing about prescreening tests for $150. We had done this years before, but his doctor said they were not necessary because they were not that extensive, and you still would have to do the main tests anyway. I asked him a couple of times if he was sure that he didn't want us to do them, and he said no. There was one in particular that might have been useful in this situation to indicate that there may be a problem.

Looking back, there were potential heart warning signs over several years that may have been indicators but didn't seem that important at the time.

Gary took some Tums a few times that last month for indigestion which he never really had. He had been coughing his head off every morning for about six weeks, almost throwing up the last day or two of his life. He saw his doctor a few days before he died, and the doctor ordered a chest x-ray for potential residual bronchitis. He had that x-ray the day before he died. In fact, we were looking at the results within a few hours before he died. The results showed a bit of scar tissue or infection in the bottom of his lungs, but nothing that serious.

He had had a few times of chest tightness that he said felt different than anything before, but it only lasted a few minutes. Also, a few times over a few years, his right foot and ankle were swollen for a while. A couple of times for a little while he said his arm felt numb, and he felt like his arm was useless. He had low energy and felt bad sometimes but never missed work.

None of these things lasted long, and to both of us, these signs did not seem to point to anything that serious. In fact, I kept thinking to myself that if I went to the doctor every time I had something irregular or an ache or pain, I would have to live beside the doctor's office.

On the day he died, he wanted me to put out a sign on the lawn for a fundraiser. He just didn't feel good, and he had never said that before. Shortly after that, I suggested that he see a cardiologist and he asked, "Why would you say that?"

I replied, "The doctors you are going to have not figured this out, so maybe another doctor would have a new idea."

He said that it took too long to get an appointment, and he wanted to let his doctor finish his line of thinking.

I suggested that we make an appointment anyway, and eventually, he would see the doctor. The appointment didn't happen.

I had looked up heart symptoms and thought maybe there was something there. I feel sure that he knew too. I just hesitated to bring it up.

Did my hesitation cause my husband's death?

REFLECTION ON LOSING YOU

July 9, 2017 – Five months after death

First of all, let's get something straight: I'll never get over it. It is ridiculous to think that anyone "gets over" a traumatic loss in their life. I hope to learn to live with it in such a way that it becomes a part of my life and not the sad dominating factor of my life. Right now it is an external event that is squeezing me lifeless, pounding me into the ground, smothering me at every turn.

Why would anyone even expect someone to just move on and forget about it? YOU NEVER FORGET!!

Would you ask someone to just forget about their deceased beloved mother or best friend? I hope not.

I did not want to lose my husband. I never saw it coming. It has been a little over 5 months now. On August 3, it will be 6 months. At that 6 month mark, if I have not awakened from this nightmare, and he has not returned, I will admit (at least I think I will) that he is gone. I will take the military marker from my living room to the cemetery to be placed on the grave since I will finally be admitting defeat, loss, reality—that the love of my life really is gone.

Oh Gary, how I miss everything about you. How I wish I could have you with me again.

I love you so much.

Always and forever.

Your loving wife, 'til death us did part—and beyond

Sylvia

MY WISH

August 25, 2017 – Six months after death

I have only one wish. I wish you were here. I just want my husband back.

That's it. There is no more. Everything else that I feel and have to say emanates from that one single wish.

Oh, there are lots of other ways that I express it. For example, I may say, "I wish things were different." That means that I wish you were here. My entire life has changed, and every ounce of my belief system has been rocked to the core.

Perhaps others are not this dramatic in their view of things, but it all makes so little sense. There is no way to understand it if you have not experienced it. And I really don't want anyone else in the world ever to have to go through this. And yet, I know that they will.

I wish you were here. Such a long time ago you died. Or was it only yesterday? Either way, I still don't believe it. I have been shaken throughout my being in ways that I could never have imagined. Why did you have to go so suddenly?

I wish I could retire with you. There is no one else and nothing else that is even a close second. Yet I must find a new approach for the final moments of my life.

Some things have not changed, and won't. Our relationship was amazing. We were committed to each other. Our simple existence made the other one happy. I will love you always and forever. And I believe that you will love me always and forever too.

When I go to bed at night, the mere presence of you in bed, and my being safe and cozy with you is gone.

You know what I miss the most? When I want to tell someone something, it was always you. Now there is not a person to hear and care about my day, to know that I am on the way home in the dark and should arrive in 15 minutes, that our friend is sick and we need to go see her, that I think I mishandled something.

I do not have my constant source of advice, my confidant, my rock. Everything seems bigger than it is.

COME BACK TO ME. I miss you so much, and I want you back in my arms again.

OBSERVATIONS OF THE FIRST SIX MONTHS

August 31, 2017 – Six months after death

It has been just over six months since I lost my beloved Gary. So what are my observations? It's hard to know because it is all so new. But here are some things I think about as I think back.

- This is the worst thing that has ever happened to me, and the hardest thing I have ever done.

- People say the dumbest things with the best of intentions. (I know because I used to do it too!)

- I can't stand crowds unless I am unknown. People don't know what to say, and I don't know what to tell them to say.

- I always drive because I might have to leave suddenly, without warning.

- I fall apart for no apparent reason, or over something that has nothing to do with my reaction.

- I am okay being alone. However, I am lonely for my husband.

- I use "I" and "we" interchangeably, much the same as before he left.

- I can stay busy doing things that must be done, like the funeral and follow-up paperwork.

- I am doing most of what I do based on what my husband would think or want regarding that situation.

- I find my greatest comfort in other widows who are in my current situation, not remarried or beyond the first year of being widowed.

- I care less than ever about drama, politics, news. Period. Those things are unimportant compared to the loss of my husband.

- All beliefs and faith that I had have been shaken.

- One of the first things I wondered is why we fiddle around with murderers on death row while my husband—the best of the best—died.

- I feel that there is no one who would have or would ever give me the unconditional love I received from my husband.

- I am totally self-centered. All the people around me will have to fend for themselves over this loss and other things. I am dealing with myself first, foremost, and almost exclusively.

- I don't know how much I want to live. If faced with a questionable disease, I don't know if I would fight it or not.

- I am tired of being told how good I look, how they are glad to see me out having fun, how I'm such a strong person. Don't they know that every day I am either on autopilot or forcing myself to get ready, put one foot in front of the other, and show up for life?

- I am grateful that my husband left things so that I can basically stay the same and not have to give up everything.

- I am grateful we had almost 34 years of marriage and that he loved me unconditionally.

- I am thankful that for many years I experienced the best kind of love with my husband.

- I am grateful that I had the ideal extended family for eight years. My mother and father above me, my husband and brother beside me, and my son and daughter below me.

- I am doing things, sometimes okay, sometimes half-heartedly. I have not totally committed to living yet. If I die, I will be where Gary is, I hope.

- I have solidified who my primary support friends are. I have found some well-meaning friends to be too intense.

- I tune out if I'm being given advice. I don't want to hear it.

- I just want my husband back. It is still possible, although only remotely possible, that I am in a bad dream or nightmare.

- I just want my husband back. Gary, I love you, always and forever.

WE DIDN'T NEED EACH OTHER

September 11, 2017 – Seven months after death

We agreed on this almost as soon as we met—we didn't need each other. Both Gary and I had satisfying professional lives, decent homes, nice friends—life was good for both of us. Yes, we agreed that we didn't need each other. More than anything, we WANTED each other.

Need is an interesting concept. How much fun it was to each have two lives—the life of an individual and the life of a couple. As humans, we work hard to fulfill our needs. We engage services, resources, jobs, recreation, intellectual pursuits, and yes, people, to fulfill our needs. Too many couples we knew had lives that dissolved into one, and they lost their individual identities. For example, if you need money and the new relationship takes care of that need, when there is enough money later, the initial basis for the relationship is gone, and there may or may not be another reason for sustaining it.

We just wanted each other. Even though we had fun on our own, we had more fun together. Even though each was self-confident, we supported, encouraged, and lifted each other to new heights. Although we enjoyed our independence, together we meshed our lives to enjoy and challenge each other. We were tight. We were often inseparable. Our togetherness was calm and exciting, relaxing and stimulating, yet motivating and satisfying all at the same time.

Just to discuss things—the workday, news, children, movies, new carpet—all of it was hugely satisfying on so many levels. What we enjoyed the most was having the company of another who really knew and understood, well, everything. We had friends and family but having each other—that was really special.

Our triad was as it should be—a solid three-legged stool that was Gary, Sylvia, and the couple. We respected each other as individuals and partners in the marriage. How much fun we each had leading the double life of an individual and a couple at the same time. When he died, my life lost two-thirds of the triad's foundation.

In the spirit of the strength of how our relationship began thirty-four years earlier, meaning that of wanting each other, I am reeling from his sudden death. However, some things are still the same. I have my own individuality. We each had carefully respected and preserved our own selves. This means I will survive the logistics required in this life—paying bills, hiring contractors, buying cars, traveling, visiting friends and family, and all other daily parts of life—because I had those skills and experiences both before and during our marriage.

Love is an interesting thing. We defined it in our own way, as others do, but mostly it represented the merging of two individuals to each become a better version of themselves.

We didn't need each other—we WANTED each other. And that defined the height, width, and depth of our love.

WE HAD A PERFECT MARRIAGE

September 11, 2017 – Seven months after death

Our marriage was perfect. Yes, I guess that most people don't believe there is any such thing as a perfect marriage. But ours was.

A perfect marriage is one that experiences and survives everything—absolutely everything. The good, the bad, and the ugly.

Our relationship had its share of ups and downs. And for us, it was good or in the pursuit of good, so that we defined it as all good.

We had some very romantic and exciting adventures, and we had some difficult challenges and obstacles.

When we first met, Gary and I couldn't stand being apart. He said that we would do everything together, including going to the grocery store. Indeed, we did go the grocery store together a lot!

One thing we both really looked forward to for years was our biweekly "Dump Date." This was when we took trash to the dump, threw it in together, talked the ten minutes there and back and called it quality time, without children, animals, and phones to distract us.

A perfect marriage has its problems, and we too had our share of internal and external challenges.

A simple dilemma involved our desires to live in our own home states. We compromised by living in his South Dakota and my North Carolina, as well as Washington, DC and south Florida. There were advantages and disadvantages to all the moves, but the main goal was always to just be together.

The biggest challenge was having a family. Seven of our first eight years brought infertility disappointments and expenses that included operations, shots, procedures, and multiple doctors, costing tens of thousands of dollars on a gut-wrenching emotional roller coaster.

That journey concluded with the ultimate adoptions of Michael from Peru and Marisa from Paraguay. The long and tedious journey was worth the end abundance of joy. We couldn't imagine life any other way.

Because we had committed to being together, various aspects of our lives were minimized or maximized but not marginalized. Everything worked out, and our perfect marriage included conversation, conflict, compromise, caring, concern, and most of all Unbridled and Unconditional Love.

SNAPSHOT OF A MOMENT–SOME DAYS I DON'T WANT TO LIVE

December 9, 2017, 8:21 a.m. – Ten months after death

I haven't fully decided if I want to live or not. Ten months after my husband dropped dead beside me without warning, life is without meaning. No, I am not going to actively try to take my life. It's just that I'm so calm when I hear about death that it surprises me.

If something might shave a few years off my life, I say okay.

If I'm supposed to do something for long-term gain, I'm thinking I might not be here 60 seconds from now so what difference does it make.

When I used to think about death, I didn't want any part of it. Now that my husband has died, it is more real to me as a part of the continuum of life. I'm so calm when someone is dying or very sick and might not make it that I do not know if it is acceptance or denial.

I don't know what I think about these perspectives. This is just an observation of the current reaction.

———

At each stage, I could not imagine things ever being different. However, my changing landscape of life did show growth and new perspectives that became obvious only after I read these entries later.

MY CHANGING LANDSCAPE

June 14, 2017 – Four months after Gary's death

I loved my old life. So busy, often stressed, a bit crazy at times keeping up with things, but happy with what we had to do and what we wanted to do.

I reflected on my life with Gary and saw a vision of a landscape with lots of clumps of trees in endless woods and meadows. I saw us each day planning the order in which we would individually and together tackle the task residing in each clump of trees by determining the paths to follow.

Tasks included a doctor's appointment, pick up the kids, go to work, have lunch together, and buy a birthday card in between. Just the normal tasks of a family of four. Sometimes our paths would cross at some trees, and we would do those things together. Some things we each did on our own. Such was life in our positive and active landscape setting.

Then I pondered my life today, four months after his death. Now, however, I look out and see a bright white landscape of flat sand. It goes in all directions, and I am the only one standing there. There is nothing on the landscape. Nothing is on the horizon, just nothing. No trees to go to. It is neither happy nor sad, just existing, both me and the landscape around me. I cannot even begin to decide where to go and what to do, and I can't tell how far the end is, or even if there is an end to the sand.

I feel totally lost. So I just stand there.

August 26, 2017 – Six months after death

It has been six months since Gary's death. My landscape has changed, but only slightly. Today when I look out over the landscape, I see some little scattered domes. They are not white, so they do not appear to be sand dunes. They are not green like vegetative growth. They are more grayish, not colorful, and they are in front of me. I cannot tell what they are, or how far away. There is no sense of good or bad, happy or sad. Just a general interest I have that something is there. Perhaps these are the various aspects of my life as I struggle to make decisions. I am a long way from clarity of any type, but I am aware of a few little changes. Like the way this landscape looks. But changes so slight that I can't really define them.

I see my life as some moments of pleasure against a backdrop of profound sadness. When something is fun, I am reminded in very short order that it is a fleeting feeling, and not the norm. For example, I may have a nice lunch with a friend. But the enjoyment ends, not when I get home, but the moment I walk out of the restaurant. Typically, I would call my husband to tell him about the lunch, discuss the rest of the day, and chat about other aspects of our lives. Quickly now the joy is gone, and sadness takes its place.

I guess I should be encouraged that there are moments that I do enjoy. Perhaps this is a step forward. Perhaps these are my domes in the sand. I hope that in my landscape eventually I will SEE trees that are alive and thriving, SMELL the fresh green grass, HEAR the joyful noises of nature, FEEL the warm sun on my face, and experience a zest for living that is so vibrant I can TASTE it.

I don't know yet. I have never walked this path before.

January 3, 2018 – Eleven months after death

At eleven months after Gary's death, I have looked over my landscape, and it has changed somewhat. It has gone from a barren landscape to a few unidentifiable mounds in the sand, to a lot of mounds in the sand. I cannot tell what they are, I have no feeling of good or bad, happy or sad, related to them. But there are a lot of them!

Perhaps these are the many things that I need to do, might do, could do. Perhaps these include the things I have, had, might have. Maybe some are people. But I cannot tell what any of the mounds are, just that somehow my landscape is changing.

September 27, 2020 – Three and a half years after death

As I look out over my landscape today, it has changed dramatically. It is active and interesting, colorful and vibrant. There are buildings that represent the many aspects of my life, and others that house information about things that I may or may not pursue. The country in the distance is lush and alive. It calls my name to be a part of it too.

The atmosphere feels light and airy. It is fresh and comfortable. It feels like hope flows freely.

7
YEAR ONE AND STILL MORE DOING THE GRIEF – DEEP THINKING

YEAR ONE THINKING WAS RANDOM, SUPERFICIAL YET DEEP, AND CONFUSING.

I DON'T CARE IF I LIVE OR DIE

Following Gary's death, my immediate feeling was that I didn't want to live. I didn't care if I lived or died. If I had needed treatment for some disease shortly after this death, I most likely would have refused it. It hurt to live every moment of every day.

However, I thought to myself that I was too upset and confused to organize a good suicide. I chuckle at that notion now, but there was an ounce of truth to it. And no, I would not have taken my own life. But I feel sure that I am not the only one who has felt, at least momentarily, the depths of despair that snuff out hope.

I know these dark feelings make everything seem hopeless.

And you may feel stuck or trapped. Some get counseling, busy themselves with other things, or have a personal pep talk to change their trajectory. None of these are bad options, especially seeking professional help if you think you need it.

I have always had the attitude that you do what you need to do, and "not feeling like it" is not a reason for not doing. Perhaps that came from my British mother with the stereotypical "stiff upper lip" and "carry on" attitude. Or maybe it was from my dad who had to quit school at fourteen and support the family when his dad died.

My attitude and experience is that staying in bed never helped me feel better. It made me feel worse if anything. So if I didn't feel like going to work, I went anyway. If I didn't want to do a certain household task, I would try to make myself do it anyway. The idea was that if I was already miserable, doing something else miserable didn't make me twice as miserable, but it did accomplish getting one more thing out of the way.

No, this was not always as easy as I may be making it sound here, and sometimes I could not muster the strength of mind and body to do anything. But there is no doubt that for me, doing something, anything, was far better for me when I was down.

PUBLIC IMAGE VS. PRIVATE AGONY

One of the things that I learned early on is to hide my feelings. No one wants to have a Debbie Downer around them.

It is acceptable to be ecstatically happy around others. But it is taboo to be severely depressed. Yet it takes a lot of energy to put on a happy face when you're grieving.

I am just plain tired of being two-faced. People are not

comfortable when you are honest about negative feelings, and I am not comfortable being dishonest about my feelings. I tried being completely honest. That usually ended with a flat, unresolved end to a conversation. I tried to say that I was fine, but I really couldn't even get those words out of my mouth.

For most of year one, I generally said I was okay. When a superior at my work pushed me to say I was fine, I insisted that no, I was just okay. Other people would ignore it and figure that okay meant okay.

Actually, in my case, had they asked what "being okay" meant, I would have said that it meant I am functioning, not happy overall but doing what I needed to do. It meant that I was in the process of healing from a wound that would never heal but hopefully would stop hurting so badly. It would mean that I was not feeling as perky as they'd wanted me to feel because I was still grieving in so many ways.

In some cases, I am not as much better as they think—I have simply become a better actor, better at being two-faced, better at masking my real feelings. I would love to be perfectly honest, to share with those who are asking. But I know they won't be able to understand.

In the end, I feel frustrated, like a fraud, unable to be my real self, or at least unable to be the self I am at that moment.

WHERE DID ALL THE PEOPLE GO?

It is hard to talk to the widowed. No one wants to be a part of that club. It might be catching, or bad luck, or just plain uncomfortable. And what do you say?

I saw some casual friends turn away at the grocery store to

avoid talking to me. And I remember turning away to avoid others too.

Everyone went back to their own lives, the same as Gary and I used to do after someone's death. During the events of the funeral and memorial service, I have some memories of a few encounters.

But the ones I really remember are those who thought of me in the months and years that followed the death. A card in the mail saying I'm thinking of you, a frozen chicken pie that just showed up, or an offer for coffee (whether I went or not). And I especially appreciated those who kindly mentioned my husband and a memory.

I remember some saying, "I remember how Gary loved that chair," and "Gary really took that Super Bowl seriously," and "Gary was thoughtful when he gave everyone flowers."

The most cherished were the ones who said, "I miss Gary too."

BEING THANKFUL?

I always thought that if I lost someone, I would immediately say, "I am so thankful for the time we had."

That is not what I thought when it happened.

I have even thought that I should write down all the things I should be grateful for.

But those were not the first things that I felt.

I was feeling hurt, loss, grief, disappointment, resentment, and so many other negative feelings that I could not even think about the positive.

Being thankful was a concept, not a feeling.

Throughout my whole life, I always was thankful for the family that I had, and I always had thought that the first thing I would say if I lost someone was that I am just thankful to have had him/her for that time.

That is NOT what I thought and felt after my husband died. I felt cheated out of something that was special to me.

In fact, during the first year, part of me wanted to say, "I am so grateful that I had over thirty-three years with my husband."

The reality was that I could not complete that sentence out loud or even in my mind. I would break down in hysterical crying. It took over a year before I could speak those words.

THEY THINK THEY UNDERSTAND EXACTLY HOW I FEEL

First of all, it is impossible for anyone to understand how I feel unless they too have been widowed.

A divorce, breakup, loss of friend, pet, job ... other types of losses are not the same. Yes, they have grief attached, but there is nothing like losing a significant other, so I wish they would not say they know exactly how I feel.

I knew I was in trouble with this when people immediately began talking too much. Their words were often empty.

You're strong.

You can do this.

You'll be fine.

I understand how you feel.

None of these things acknowledged that I was in total emotional chaos.

What they may understand is that I am in a dark and difficult place. It is very sad and very scary. No, they cannot be there for me whenever I need them. No one can be here the way my spouse was.

And no, it does not help for them to tell me these things as they stand beside their spouses and go home together, while I go home alone.

The widowed, those who knew my plight, said the least. They said they were sorry, they knew it would be difficult, and they would be glad to talk. Period. No pep talks. In fact, they were not the first ones to rush in my door at the time of death because they knew this was a long-term situation. The worst was yet to come.

I have to tell myself that people do not mean to be hurtful, they just don't understand. Nevertheless, I try to distance myself from those who say things that are not helpful during such a fragile time.

It is okay to ask for space when you need it. Most people will graciously accommodate you. For those who don't, you can graciously excuse yourself from the situation to get the space you need.

LET ME BE A LITTLE CRAZY

When I fell apart over something little, it probably was not a reaction to that event. It was just at that moment that I lost it because of the ongoing buildup of upset and frustration.

I drove myself to places so that I could leave when I wanted to and not be trapped. I appreciated the offers to pick me up, but many times, I would be crying by the time I got to my car to go home. I needed the space.

I sometimes would get up for no apparent reason and simply say, "I have to leave now. It has nothing to do with you and everything to do with my need to go."

I have missed events because I just couldn't go. And this has included family events.

The first Thanksgiving after Gary died, I couldn't stop crying all day. I was unable to go to the family dinner at my brother's home, just a quarter mile up the road. I missed the entire event and that evening got takeout at suppertime since I'd cried continuously and still had not eaten all day.

CUTTING COMMENTS

I believe that people are mostly well intentioned in their comments. However, they forget that in the throes of grief, the most overriding factor is your emotional devastation. And that is the very thing that they generally don't want to acknowledge. Here are a few of the examples of comments that dressed me down and cut me to the quick even though they were not intended that way.

Less than three weeks out: "Out enjoying yourself"

My children were still at home and getting ready to go back to their lives. They were going to meet some friends at a local gathering place, and they insisted I go too even though that was the last thing that I wanted to do. They didn't want to leave me home alone, and I did go and tried to put on a positive face.

I saw a friend while out, and they said, "I'm glad to see you are out having a good time."

I was speechless.

One month out: "Good things come from bad"

Less than a month after Gary's death, I was told by a person that this individual has noticed that something good always comes from something bad, so something good would come from his death. I was stunned. That was not a helpful comment for a grieving widow.

Four months out: "New normal"

A friend said calmly, "I guess you're working on your new normal." I don't even remember how I responded because all I could think was that I was barely in survival mode, and my approach to all this was not just creating a new plan of things to do.

Five months out: "God needed him"

Two people told me that God needed Gary more than I did. Without hesitation, I immediately retorted, "I don't think so. You tell God to send him back." They were shocked.

Nine months out: "Don't do deep grief"

I was devastated on the day of the anniversary of the day Gary and I met. I had been to the Veterans Day parade, which we always went to (Gary had been a Marine Corps officer). I went late, cried while there, and left early.

I planned to take myself to the restaurant that he would have taken me to. Before leaving to go to the restaurant, an acquaintance confronted me to say that this deep grief was not good for me, and I needed to get someone else.

This person had observed that people did better if they got someone else after a death or breakup or divorce, or even people who lost a dog did better if they got another one. Through this brief talk, I said stop in three different ways. I said, "I don't want to talk about it," "don't go there," and "that's enough." Because the person continued talking, I had to get up and leave. I was rattled by the insensitivity.

SUPPORTING OTHERS

I still feel some guilt about doing a lousy job of supporting others.

I was so self-absorbed over my loss that I was not there for others at all. I regret that, but I just could not muster enough energy to look outside of my own cocoon.

One day my brother said, "You're not the only one who lost someone." And he was right. Even though I agreed, I was still not much help to anyone else.

My children did not get the support from me that I believe I should have given. They were living out of town and out of state, each with a significant other, so they did have someone with them during that time. I was very grateful for that.

Gary was many things to many people. He was a model husband and father. He was also a much beloved brother, brother-in-law, nephew, cousin, and relative to so many others. He was a dear friend to the many people he met from his childhood through Marine Corps and his varied career paths. Most of his professional life was spent in the nonprofit community helping others as CEO of Hospice of Davidson County and Executive Director of Cancer Services of Davidson County.

Gary had touched a lot of lives. There were many people affected and saddened by his death. But I still had my hands full, it seemed, just dealing with me.

THANKS TO THOSE WHO HELPED

Despite all this avoidance or annoyance at others, there were many instances where people were helpful.

I extend my thanks to all of the wonderful people for everything they did to help me through the first year. Although they may not have realized it, I was appreciative for everything.

There were those who helped me with all the things to do

the first five days after death. This included keeping up with who brought what food, marking containers, making phone calls, answering the phone, returning phone calls, taking out the trash, feeding the animals, purchasing some clothes and household items, running the dishwasher, greeting friends who stopped by when I was not available, and so much more.

During the first year, there were projects I pursued that Gary and I had planned. Two rooms needed redoing from ceiling to floor. It entailed putting up sheetrock on the ceiling and walls, sanding, painting, installing new fixtures, removing carpet, sanding the floors, putting up blinds ... basically the works from ceiling to floor.

Gary and I would have started the renovations together, but by myself, I was soon in over my head. It would never have been completed if it hadn't been for my friends and neighbors helping find the right contractors and personally helping me finish all these projects.

There were three special people in particular who were there in the ways that I needed on a regular basis.

My brother called me every day for the first year and ever since to see if I was alive and surviving. If I didn't answer the phone, he came looking for me. He allowed me to vent some of my frustration. He has continued keeping up with me. He is my rock.

My beloved friend/neighbor allowed me to call or visit anytime. I would talk, nonstop stream of consciousness, while she listened without judgment. Her house was my safe house where I felt emotionally supported. I could come in and make myself at home in a cozy spot on the couch and escape from the world. That support was priceless. And she continues to support me.

Another close friend had coffee with me every month or two to check in on me. She too allowed me to talk. She also saw me at intervals, so she commented on the changes from one time to the next. That was actually helpful in my recognizing if my own perceptions seemed to be in line with other people's perceptions. Also priceless support. And we still continue to get together.

How can I repay them? I think the best way is to pay it forward. I want to be there for those I can in the most supportive ways possible.

JOURNEY TO NOWHERE

Many refer to this state of widowhood as a journey. Having traveled a lot in my life, I would agree that widowhood is a journey. Definitely the worst of my life.

When I travel, usually I have my bags packed, a destination in mind, plans for how to get there, and all the tools (passport, money, etc.) that I need along the way.

On this journey, I am taking everything I own, don't know where I am going, don't know how to get there, and don't know what I need. I am dragging everything along since I have no clear direction.

Throughout the first year, there were a few things that cleared up in a weird sort of way. For example, stops along the way in the first three months included changes in paperwork (banks, insurances, DMV, and so many more) that needed to be updated. If I didn't know what to do, someone told me. Basically I finally learned to take my file of all papers, including death certificates, with me everywhere I went.

Even at that, I was always missing something and had to go

back another time. Paperwork like this, every day, defined the first three months. However, my destination remained undefined as I just made random stops along my journey. At least, that was the way it felt.

And the journey continues.

8
YEAR TWO MUDDLING ALONG – REMEMBRANCE AND PERCEPTIONS

YEAR TWO WAS WHEN I REALIZED,
OH MY GOSH, THIS REALLY IS THE WAY IT IS GOING TO BE.

WISHING FOR A COMA

Life without Gary was inconceivable. In fact, after the first few days of shock, I felt that there was a good chance, maybe fifty-fifty, that I was in a coma and would awaken from this nightmare. I envisioned that when I woke up in the hospital, Gary would say to me, "I was the one who was having a problem, and then you fell over in a coma... what happened?"

At that very moment, I would be so grateful and so happy to relinquish all of my recent experiences as part of a bad dream and move back into blissful reality with my husband. I determined that if I had not awakened after six months that it probably was not a coma. I told a few trusted friends about this theory of mine. I didn't want the world to think I was crazy.

At about the six-month mark, a friend asked how I felt now that the six-month mark had come and gone. I said that I was still not convinced that his death was real, and I would give it till nine months or maybe a year. Eventually, a year came and went, and I was still here living and breathing on this earth.

My hope of waking up to a different reality died with the one-year anniversary of the death of my husband.

EVERYTHING IS SECOND CHOICE

I do not believe that everything happens for a reason. I believe that everything just happens, and when you lose first choice, you have to settle for second choice.

So I continue my journey to evaluate choices and select the best options for me.

Sometimes I am still asked, "Aren't you glad to get to do such-and-such now?"

The truth?

No, I just want my husband back.

Why do people want to sugarcoat a loss? It is because they find it uncomfortable to be around. And they don't understand. And they could be next.

THE WEIGHT OF GUILT

Most people feel a sense of guilt when someone dies.

The guilt is as simple as "I wish I had called last week when I thought about it" or "if I had not insisted he come, he wouldn't have been in that wreck and died."

The guilt that we impose on ourselves is almost always unwarranted, yet I continued to question what I could have done to prevent Gary's untimely death.

Maybe I have known about people who were snatched from the jaws of death at the last moment by someone else's actions. I wish that I could have had that experience.

I will never know what actions, if any, I might have taken to prevent the death. Everything about it is irreversible. I hope that I, and others who are widowed, will let the guilt slip away and concentrate our thoughts and emotions on the positive and supportive aspects of our journey through grief.

JOURNAL REFLECTION AS THE GUILT CONTINUES

Monday, July 24, 2018 – One year and five months after death

Dear Gary,

I miss you. Please come back to me. This can't be real. I love you so much. If I awake from this nightmare, we will sell this house, travel, get a modest place, quit work, and enjoy every moment of every day together. We will be together nonstop. I love you.

Do you blame me for not doing enough?

It had crossed my mind several times that maybe a heart thing was going on when the docs could not find anything else. In fact, before you died, I said that maybe you should go to a cardiologist and you quickly retorted, "Why would you say that?"

I suggested that maybe a different doctor would have an idea what was going on since the other docs couldn't find anything. I was thinking about how the orthopedic surgeon ended up being our best resource for other health issues in our family.

I should have insisted earlier—a month or so earlier when it occurred to me. When I mentioned trying different doctors, you said you already had things underway and wanted to let your current doctor follow through with his set of tests. However, I did ask that week if you had told him about your tight chest. You said no.

And I said, "Don't you think that would have been a good thing to tell him?"

You said, "I guess so."

Too little, too late. I should have insisted on getting you to a cardiologist. If you had been mad with me for interference, wouldn't that have been better than losing you altogether? I am so sorry that I did not make more of a fuss because maybe I could have made a difference.

When you once said you didn't want me to have to take care of you in sickness, I made some cryptic comment like we were married and in it for the long run. I knew that one of us would take care of the other, and we'd deal with it when we needed to.

I was not as empathetic as I could have been when you were feeling bad that day, or when you called me into the room. I had no idea you might die!

I should have called 911 immediately. I had you tell me where the doctor's number was instead of finding it myself. I sort of blanked.

I love you so much. I wish I could have a redo. I want you more than ever. Please come back. Please let this only be the worst nightmare ever from which you and I emerge so that we can enjoy our collective retirements together.

I am having trouble finding a purpose for living. The days are long and sometimes tedious. I'm just simply doing things to pass the time. I want you. I need you. I love you.

I love you. I love you. I love you.

Always and forever.

Your loving wife, Sylvia

THOUGHTS ON LIFE GENERATED BY GARY'S DEATH

I've learned a few things throughout my grief journey.

You cannot control others.

You must let your kids go at eighteen. They must enjoy both the rights **and** responsibilities of life. You only serve in an advisory position.

After someone dies, everything is different.

Forgive. Easier said than done, I know.

Say **no.**

Holding on to grief is **not** a testament to the person who died. Honoring their life and the good memories is. But I'm not there yet.

You can't control everything. Maybe you don't control anything. But you can affect many things.

If you can't beat 'em, join 'em.

You don't heal completely. You never get over it. You just keep doing a little better, hopefully. It gets better, but not on an even continuum. Some days are setbacks and relapses, but you will still come out a little ahead later.

Healing helps put it all in perspective.

There is less to regret, forgive, justify if we live in this moment.

And ultimately, personal peace needs to be the goal.

9
BUILDING MOMENTUM
FROM THE PAST

YES, THINGS CHANGE AND PERCEPTIONS CHANGE.
NOTHING MAKES SENSE UNTIL IT IS ALL OVER AND
YOU ARE LOOKING BACK.

Year three began a transition that was so marked that even I noticed it. There were fewer tears less often. There were also fewer freak-outs and greater awareness of the life around me.

It was not until year three that I could really look back and see what had happened, and how it all had affected me. There are many things that are still unfinished business for me. But year three did give me some clarity.

For one thing, I was crying less. That was big. It meant that I was accepting my new day-to-day routine in a calmer way. It meant that I was spending less energy on the grieving process. And it meant that I was more comfortable going places and meeting people.

It meant that I was creating a new life.

Don't get me wrong. It was not that I was leaving my life with

Gary behind. Quite the opposite. He continues to be a part of my daily life. I often think of him and talk to him and consult with him. I often feel his presence.

And even though life feels a little smoother, I would trade everything just to have him back again. So don't confuse my acknowledging relief from grief and repositioning my life without him to be me letting go.

Actually, I am doing what almost all who are widowed eventually do. I am taking him along in new ways.

It is like a train that is slowly rambling through the country, making occasional brief stops to let people on and off. When people once again embark the train, they may have different luggage or at least they have repacked in new ways.

That is me. Everything is coming with me in my baggage for the trip. As I look at my baggage, I have recognized some profound changes in how and what I pack. Some things are close to the top of the bags because they are part of my everyday life. Some are packed further down because they are not needed as often. Much of the negative is tucked into the corners and pockets out of sight so it does not intrude on my everyday life. But now I get to decide what new things will fill up my bag for future adventures.

And that's what this chapter is all about—how I built momentum for the future from the reflections of the past.

DOING WHAT I HAD TO DO

There were so many things that I had to do after Gary's death. I wrote down each thing as I thought of it. (Then, of course, I had to find the notes!)

For the first three months, I went every day to try and

complete something. I say try because there was usually a problem. I didn't have the right documents, the right person wasn't there, it required going another place first, and so on. I quickly learned that everything would take longer than I thought.

One example that I vividly recall was with the NC Department of Motor Vehicles. This was a most tedious process. What should have taken a trip or two to the DMV ended up being many trips over several months.

We owned two trailers and five vehicles, all old but running well. I went to get everything put in my name, take his name off some papers, and so on. I found that I had to change everything to one name. Sounds easy, right? Wrong.

From high school age on, I always thought that I would keep my maiden name. I always thought, and still do, that a woman shouldn't be flagging her marital status at work by changing names. So I kept my name for business and added Drake to it for family. Well, I sort of did that.

My name was Sylvia Anette Walters. I left my passport alone since it is renewed only once every ten years. I kept my name at work and on my credit cards. I changed my name with Social Security and on my driver's license to Sylvia A. Walters Drake. There was an issue when I had to show my ID with my credit card. It was always questioned.

So I had switched the driver's license back to Sylvia Annette Walters. Whenever I booked a hotel room, did I do it in Drake or Walters? I could never remember. I just learned to give both names everywhere and they could figure it out.

The NC Department of Motor Vehicles didn't see it that way. When I showed up with titles for the five vehicles and two trailers, the primary names were Gary M. Drake, Sylvia A. Walters, Sylvia A. Walters Drake, Sylvia A. Drake, and another one or two. I had to go to the Clerk of Court to have all of my aliases put in one document because according to the DMV, all vehicles had to all be in the same name.

This time is another example of me not knowing what I didn't know. While grieving and still trying to function, I had to spend extra time and energy to resolve things. The DMV changes required extra trips to the Courthouse several times.

In fact, nothing was simple. But in three months, I got most of the documents at various institutions in good order. (Truth is, after the three-year mark, there are still some documents and other paperwork that have not yet been completed.)

KEEPING MY JOB

When Gary died, I was teaching at a local community college. And I did not leave my job.

Oh, there were miserable days that I didn't want to go to work or anywhere else. However, I went in anyway. In my case, I mostly stuck with the tasks at hand and was able to complete my work as usual. There were a few times when I simply got stuck and couldn't think and complete some paperwork or something. My supervisor and colleagues jumped in and helped me get over those humps.

I did have the clarity of mind to remember my philosophy about being miserable. First, if you feel like doing nothing, you might as well be doing something. You'll actually accomplish something that you wouldn't have to do later.

Second, if you are already miserable and you do something you don't like or you don't want to do, you are not going to be twice as miserable. And you may actually end up feeling a little better for having accomplished something. Eventually I found joy in working again and appreciated the mental reprieve while engaging with my students.

FULFILLING TRAVEL DREAMS

As I look back, I am proud of myself for meeting personal travel goals. These were personal goals that I had for me and us before Gary's death. It was not a small thing to take off on my own in some of these circumstances. But it wasn't just that I wanted to go to these places. I had a burning desire to go, each for a different reason.

The first summer alone, three months after Gary's death, I flew to England and returned home three weeks later. I needed a group hug, and I got it there.

You see, my mother was English. She was a war bride after meeting my dad during WWII in England. All of her relatives are in England, so that was the place to go. It was a healing trip that also included fun. I cried most days and regretted that I was without my husband on the trip. We were planning to visit England before Gary died.

The second summer after, I fulfilled a personal goal. I left for six weeks. The first nine days, I was with a group of students in Greece and Italy. Then I flew to Nepal and stayed for several weeks, toured a week in Tibet, and spent my last four days in India.

Many years ago as a new college graduate, I had lived six months in Nepal on a cultural exchange program. I loved it and always said I left a piece of my heart there. I always knew that I would go back to find it.

In Nepal, I had arranged through a friend to be a guest lecturer at the University of Kathmandu, which was something that I had wanted to do for a while. I was based in the capital of Kathmandu and toured the city as well as other parts of the country.

Part of that heart journey included my interest in Tibetan refugees who I'd found out about all those years ago in Nepal. I visited two refugee camps in Nepal, befriended several street vendors, traveled overland to Llasa, Tibet, to see the original home of the Dalai Lama, and visited Dharamshala to visit the Dalai Lama's current home.

It was a wonderful personal journey. Was I lonely? Yes, I missed my husband, but I had new friends and kept my focus on appreciating and enjoying the trip.

By the third summer, I was fulfilling a dream that Gary and I had. I purchased a truck and 18-foot trailer for a cross-country trip. I left by myself and traveled twenty-four states and 11,300 miles in nine weeks.

I visited ten national parks, many state parks, national monuments and forests, friends in Texas and Montana and family in South Dakota, toured, ate, wrote in my journal, and so much more. I camped in public and private campgrounds and made many changes in plans along the way.

I had two signs in my windows that read: Gary M. Drake Memorial Cross-Country Trip. Part of it was a trip we probably would have made together, part of it was my own personal interests. In any event, it was a great time. There were some sad tears still but not as many as previous years.

TO MOVE OR NOT TO MOVE

I was amazed at the number of people who expected me to sell my house, auction off many of our belongings, and move somewhere else. Being in good health and of sound mind (at least, I think), it was not a consideration. This, after all, was still my home. However, staying meant taking care of things.

I have worked to make the house comfortable for just me. A widowed friend of ours told me that he enjoyed his house, but it took three years to get it all the way he wanted it. I thought to myself, *That is too long.*

In reality, it took me over three years to start feeling comfortable in the house. I hesitated to change some things because that was, in my mind, part of dismantling the relationship with Gary.

I didn't want to move the picture that he loved from the wall. I didn't mind moving the table to a different room since I had been talking about that before he died. And without hesitation I moved my office and supplies to new areas because it was practical for me. It was a gradual change. Eventually, I felt more comfortable in my home, enjoying the things around me, and feeling like I wanted a friend or two to stop in.

PERSONAL GOALS

As soon as my husband died, I had a flood of personal goals related to him that leaped to the surface.

The first had to do with having the type of funeral and memorial service that would most appropriately honor the very essence of his being. I personally attended to every detail so that everything had meaning.

After the first week activities ended and everyone went home, I made a new list. I chose to write every single thank you to everyone so that I could put a personal sentence in each one. It took me a few months to get them all completed.

I found every picture we had taken during his last year and put them in an album so that nothing would be lost.

I started new files for all the personal sympathy cards and other items related to the funeral, his life, and his death.

I made contributions in memory of Gary to his favorite charities.

I tried my best to keep things going with the house, bills, yard, cars, and everything else the way he would have done it.

Over the three years, though, things changed. I started to make some decisions about new ways of doing things partly because, with only one person, needs are just different.

In the beginning, these changes underscored the fact that I was alone, and they made me feel lonely. As time has passed, I have accepted them as practical with little thought. Now some of the decisions are my own personal preference, and I feel satisfaction in selecting things I want.

As I move forward, I have made new plans. I intend to travel more, both domestically and internationally. I plan to switch careers to writing, speaking, and training. I will spend more time with my children and close friends and family. I expect to be basking in more lazy moments, savoring both the simpler and finer things in life. And I will reflect on the fond memories and rich experiences that have brought me to this stage of life.

10

Tips for the Widowed – Surviving and Thriving

How do you handle grief?
Here are a few insights and food for thought.

HOW TO PROCEED

There is no one right way to grieve. While we all have some similarities, we have many differences. Some of my reactions and comments may seem too simplistic, or unrealistic, or unrelatable. The bottom line is that the right way is whatever works for **you**, and what is good for **you**.

There are many books and resources that you can read to better understand the phases of grief. The main thing is that you not let the book or other people, or my writings here, affect what you believe to be the right thing for you. **You** are the only one who should be making a decision about what is right.

For anyone who is struggling, take one day, or hour, or even moment at a time. Whatever helps you. I will say that some days I could actually think ahead to the next day, but mostly it was all I could do to have a semi-plan for the things that **had** to be done that day. If things were optional, then I mostly didn't do them.

The goal for me was survival. Nothing fancy, nothing organized. In fact, it was often downright ugly.

In my fourth year post-loss, things are opening up in the world. I am starting to see that the world has so many options. I am selecting the things that support me. I am pushing aside those things that try to bring me down.

I am beginning to live again, breathe, relax, enjoy, appreciate... and sometimes thrive.

EVER-PRESENT THOUGHTS AND FEELINGS

Some thoughts persist and linger. Some of them we want to lose as fast as we can, and some things we want with us for the rest of our lives. Here were some of my thoughts.

- Those people who think they know how it feels (but don't) have a good chance of eventually being widowed too.

- I feel hurt and jealous sometimes seeing other couples enjoying each other as Gary and I used to.

- I feel irritated when I hear someone talking trash about their spouse.

- My husband is just as present as if he were still alive. It is as if he went to the store and is a long time coming back.

- Grief has been my whole life some days, and I know it will always be a part of my life.

- I guess this grief is the price I paid for that love.

- Some things can't be fixed.

- Some wounds don't heal.

- I can have grief and love at the same time.

WE DON'T MOVE ON–WE MOVE ALONG

I am always amazed about how people think that we move on from one thing to another in life, leaving things behind as if they no longer affect us.

The truth is that we don't move on. **We move along.**

Time is like a slow-moving walkway, or a really slow-moving train that never stops and just keeps going. We are the passengers, taking what we need and want, leaving some things along the way as we repack for the next part of the journey. Even if we leave some things behind, we still take the memories and impacts they made on us. Those things stay with us forever.

I know that my focus during year one was simply survival. That was a big job for me.

By year two, I focused on accepting that it would never be the same again and realized that I would eventually revive myself and my life from the shambles.

In years three and four, a new future started to come into focus. As I finish this book, I am just beginning to thrive in living from the lessons of the past, and I feel hopeful for the future.

Being widowed means that we must repackage our lives. Even if we don't want to, part of it has already been done to and for us. In fact, most of our activities, perceptions, priorities, and sometimes our beliefs change. We have the chance to make things be somewhat less uncomfortable, depending on how we repackage things.

Sometimes the widowed are encouraged to do something. The truth here is that we **are** doing something all the time, even if it is staying in bed all day.

We did not choose what happened to us, but we can choose what we do about it from this day forward. It is an individual thing as to how many miles pass before we begin the tiniest changes, and what changes we choose to make along the way.

IT IS NOT EASY. That is why baby steps are required. The tiniest thing you do differently today or tomorrow is cause for a major "way to go!" So congratulate yourself on each little thing.

YOU CAN RELY ON ONLY YOURSELF FOR SURVIVAL

In December 2017, almost a year after losing Gary, I visited a widowed friend of mine. We had not seen each other since before her husband died, and he had been gone more than twelve years.

I expected some soft touches and encouraging words. She has always been honest and real with me, and one of the first things that she said is that you have to rely on yourself. There is no one else. She repeated it that day until I got it. Her four children and my two children had their own lives. They were not there for the daily activities and decisions, or for the nightly depression in the endless nights. NO ONE was there. That is the way it was.

Early on for most who are widowed, there is no one else.

You are not number one in anyone's life.

No one can or will be there for you all the time the way your spouse was.

Hard words to hear. But true. And I got the message.

I didn't like to hear it then, and I cringe to hear it now. But I know that it means when I look around and no one is there, that I must act on my own.

Sometimes I do better than other times. But I got the message. I am me, and I am alive, and I am responsible for myself. Whether I like it or not.

I also got the message that things can and will change for the better.

LOVE YOUR SPOUSE'S BEST FRIEND

- Your spouse loved you.

- Figure out why, and love yourself for the same reasons.

- Your spouse would want you to find peace and comfort.

- You need to work on finding peace and comfort.

- You are now your own best friend.

- Your spouse would be very upset if you were not taking care of your own best friend.

- And that is your responsibility now.

EXPLORING YOUR PLAN TO SURVIVE, REVIVE, AND THRIVE

The goal of year one is just to survive—to do those things for yourself that will assure that you do survive. You are not in the best thinking mode, so it is best to slow down and be gentle with yourself.

So how did I survive? After someone passes away, your life becomes a blank slate. A friend of mine told me to always have something to look forward to in the next day or so. It didn't have to be big. Call a friend. Meet for coffee. Send a card. Watch a favorite movie (alone or with someone), visit your kids/neighbor/anyone. Whether you choose to involve someone else in your small action is up to you.

At one point, my main thing to do was put something in the dishwasher in the morning and afternoon. Not much, but it was an accomplishment beyond the things that had to be done. It made me feel better.

My goal in general was to survive the first year, start to revive my life the second year, and strive to thrive in the third and fourth years.

I decided that I needed to be doing something. Here are some things I thought about to begin to help myself come out of this funk.

1. WHAT TO DO.

Think about things to do. For example, taking out the trash.

Stop doing anything and everything if you don't want to. There were days that I did well to have a bite to eat.

Slow down. It is okay to slow down the pace of life. I usually felt that I was accomplishing nothing because grief takes a lot of energy. But slowing down was what I needed.

Select non-threatening activities. I found that I eventually could go to certain stores that I had enjoyed with my husband, but there were others that upset me, and I had to avoid them.

Control your interactions. When I was going somewhere with anyone, I insisted on driving myself and meeting them there rather than being given a ride. I wanted and needed to be able to leave at any moment if I felt uncomfortable, and sometimes I did leave early.

Select your interactions. I cancelled some things at the last minute and explained that I just couldn't do it that day.

2. HOW TO DO IT.

I considered what the procedure would be. If my small task was to take out the trash, I would gather all the trash the night before. Then I'd take it out the next morning before coffee.

Do not complicate each day. Some days were rough, and I planned and tried to do only one or two little things, like washing dishes, and added more things on other days.

Do only what you can. I had a hard time at first being gentle with myself and giving myself to permission to do as little as possible. But it's important to not be hypercritical of yourself.

Do what you want to. And don't do the nonessential things unless you want to. Sometimes just getting out of bed was enough.

Be protective of your time to grieve, cry, or even smile about some of your best memories. Although I was sad, both alone and with others, sometimes I just had to be left alone to process things. I made sure that happened.

Find a safe spot in your home. Have the things there that help give you comfort. I lived for years, both before and after his death, on one corner of the couch across from his chair. I had papers, snacks, books, magazines, pillows, a blanket, TV remote, and other things within reach. The TV, fireplace, and his picture were across from me.

Make only the financial decisions that you have to. Now is not the time to blow through your money or make hasty purchases. I wasted $500 on a new vacuum that I simply did not need; I regretted buying it. However, I simply refused to touch other money that I had except for the usual and reasonable expenditures.

Be your own best friend. Make the decision that you will take care of yourself. The fact that you don't feel like doing it does not mean that you should ignore your own health and needs.

Give and get hugs. If you are fortunate enough to have people around who will hug you, hug them the most. I had very few since I was living alone. I think I relied on my pets for hugs, and especially Gary's pillow which I hugged and talked to every day for over a year.

Seek stability. While you are grieving, there are still things that you can be doing to help you stabilize. I was still working and made a point of keeping up with the work, whether I wanted to or not. Keeping bills paid was something I hated doing, but it kept there from being other problems, like electricity being cut off.

Give yourself flexibility. Consider little things that you might do, and leave it open as to whether you do them or not. I might think about someone I should call for their birthday, but I tried to not beat myself up if I felt unable to make the call. I sometimes would send a card or text because I just didn't feel like talking.

Talk to and spend time with safe people. I found that the best people were not always who I thought they would be. I often related to friends from the past and new friends that I met who were also widowed.

Stay away from people (including friends and family) who are not supportive. There were friends of mine who I had to minimize contact with that first year because of various things: they ignored my loss, they thought they knew exactly how I felt, they were aggressive about how I should feel, and/or they expected me to act a certain way.

Protect your time and energy. Know that it is okay to minimize time with people who are not good for you at that point in time. Some of them didn't want to be supportive or didn't know how. I chose not to spend time with them. In some cases, we were able to reconnect later.

3. HOW I FEEL WHEN THE TASK IS DONE.

Everything that you do has some feeling attached to it. Think about the positive feelings that you will have at the time you are doing a task or after it has been completed.

My task-related feelings have included satisfaction, relief, contentment, joy, weight off my shoulders, and so many more. And anticipating these feelings helps us to move along. Even if you are doing tasks that you really don't want to do, or you are doing them half-heartedly, there is usually a better feeling when they are done.

I dislike personal paperwork. Even paying a few bills is something I do grudgingly. Yet when it's done, I always feel relief that it's out of the way for another month.

When I have a social obligation, I may go and stay the whole time or half an hour or only five minutes. Even if it is not the greatest time, there was some reason I went, like maybe to wish a friend "Happy Birthday." I'm always glad I went even if the visit was brief.

Sometimes our negative feelings may get the best of us. Just remember that you shouldn't make any major changes during the time of deep grieving, especially in the first year of being widowed, unless you absolutely have to. Instead, focus on the small tasks and the positive feelings they can bring you.

I thought about moving, changing everything in the house, going on shopping sprees, traveling and never coming back, and giving away everything. I did some of these things, but always within reason. I chose the reasonable responses or actions when I considered the spectrum of feelings that I would experience.

I encourage you to think about your future feelings with any actions you take, and seek the good, positive reactions. It is a healthy distraction. And hopefully you begin to train yourself to think more positively overall.

MOVING ALONG

As you move along, keep your life as simple and safe as you can. You will become stronger and more capable of everything as time goes by. The adjustments and the grieving in the beginning are draining, but things will improve.

Here is what I did early on.

First, I would think of just one activity to do the next day.

Second, I would figure out how to do it. After all, there are several ways to get something done. For example, paying a bill may mean writing a check and mailing the payment, writing a check and taking it to the drive-through, driving yourself, or asking someone to drop it off for you, or paying the bill online.

Third, think about how you feel **before** doing it (dreading it, unsure and need help, don't mind it) and how you will feel **after** it is done (usually relieved, satisfaction at accomplishing something, happy to have it taken care of).

As you are moving along, you will survive, begin to revive, and head toward thriving again in your own world.

THE TOMORROW PLAN

As I was wanting to get a little more done, I started using my Tomorrow Plan. This helped me to address three areas of action: things that I MUST do, things that I NEED to do, and things that I WANT to do.

The **MUST** do category includes those required things we really don't want to do, but we have to do them. They may include pay the bills, get gas, call the plumber, contact the return desk, inquire about the medical bill, cancel the subscription, and so on. You usually feel relief when they are done.

The **NEED** to do category includes activities you can put off but really you want to get to them eventually. They may include activities like vacuum the room, water the plants, read the article, call a friend, buy the present, help the neighbor, write the grocery list, and so much more. You may really not want to do them, but you usually feel better and perhaps have a sense of accomplishment when they are done.

The **WANT** to do category is strictly about what brings you pleasure, whether it is for a fleeting moment or for hours. This may include decorating a table, lunch with a trusted friend, writing a letter, watching a favorite movie, going for a ride, petting your dog ... large and small activities all count here. Remember this is something you do each day just for enjoyment.

Once you determine WHAT you will do, decide HOW it will be done. Will you drive there to pick it up, go with a friend, have it delivered? Will you sip coffee while waiting on hold for customer service, gather all the paperwork before asking about the medical tests, look up prices to see which store to go to for that much-needed mattress?

Finally, think about how you will FEEL, or how you would like to feel, after it is completed. Our feelings of relief, satisfaction, and enjoyment, just to name a few, are often the motivators that get us going.

Most days, I wrote down three things that I would do the next day. This may seem very simple on the surface, but it was often hard. Heck, there were some days that planning tomorrow seemed too much. There were days I jotted down less, or more, than is indicated here. (And there days that I didn't do it at all!)

Here is an example of a Tomorrow Plan:

1. Something that I **MUST** do: Pay the electric bill
    Here's how: Write a check and mail it
    Then I will feel: Relieved when it is done

2. Something that I **NEED** to do: Wash dishes
    Here's how: Put a dish or two in the dishwasher every time I walk by
    Then I will feel: A brighter spirit from a cleaner kitchen

3. Something that I **WANT** to do: Buy a plant for the entry
    Here's how: Drive to the Garden Center tomorrow to get it
    Then I will feel: Uplifted by the colors and smell

Following is a sample of the Tomorrow Plan form. Only complete what you want. This is not so much about whether you write every detail down as that you are thinking about things to do tomorrow and you have a little plan.

Get a copy of the complete week of the Tomorrow Plan here: www.widowedinaheartbeat.com

MY TOMORROW PLAN
For this week

ACTIVITIES	SUN	MON	TUE
I **MUST** do this: Here's how: Then I will **FEEL**:			
I **NEED** to do this: Here's how: Then I will **FEEL**:			
I **WANT** to do this: Here's how: Then I will **FEEL**:			

www.widowedinaheartbeat.com

11
WHAT TO SAY AND DO
– SUGGESTIONS FOR
FAMILY AND FRIENDS

EVERYONE WANTS TO SAY AND DO THE RIGHT
THINGS.

Here are a few tips to better support your widowed friends.

Friends and family often do not know what to say or do if they have never been widowed. Those who have are different, and each one reacts differently depending on where they are in their journey. Sometimes the same comment may be accepted and appreciated, and at another time, it may be upsetting.

Following are the things that I found helpful as I processed my loss.

PLEASE DO NOT SAY THIS

There are some things that I don't want you to say when I am heartbroken, partly because these things do not address my emotions, partly because they are rude, or partly because you cannot prescribe what is best for me. Here are some of the comments I heard followed by what went through my mind.

- You're strong. You can do this. (*I did not choose this!*)

- It'll be fine. (*Really? How?*)

- We're always here for you for anything. (*I have found that you are busy too.*)

- You'll find someone else. (*This is not what I want.*)

- Everything happens for a reason. (*REALLY?*)

- God needed him more than you did. (*Well, you can just tell God to send him back.*)

- God needed another angel. (*I think the Bible indicates that angels are a different entity.*)

- Good things always come out of bad things. (*This may be what you think, but it's not helpful to say to me now.*)

- You should move on and date someone. (*Clearly, you have no idea what I am going through at this moment.*)

- Just tell me what you need. (*Although there is nothing wrong with saying this, I assure you that simply breathing is all I can manage early on. I have no idea what I need.*)

- I know exactly how you feel. (*Unless you too are widowed, you have no idea!*)

PLEASE SAY AND DO THIS

Here is a quick preview of what you should say and do to be the most helpful and supportive. Explanations and examples follow this initial list.

- Acknowledge my emotions.

- Say things that show your concern.

- Follow up with caring gestures.

- Keep the memories alive.

- Support the new lifestyle.

- Listen with love.

ACKNOWLEDGE MY EMOTIONS!

I cannot really think about other things if I have not had a chance to talk about my situation, mainly my feelings. If you really want to help, let me talk in a safe, nonjudgmental environment. Don't tell me how you want me to be. Listen to me. Let me express how I am at this time.

So remember that it's okay, actually wonderful, if you just listen!

Remember that it's about the grieving person, not you. Silence can be your best friend. And the truth is not always helpful. Acknowledge the emotions.

SAY THINGS THAT SHOW YOUR CONCERN

You can always start by saying, "I know that you are hurting." Then mention my spouse and a little memory. Even if I get tears in my eyes, I want to talk about him or her. I want to hear about him or her. I want to know that someone else misses him or her.

Other kind things to show concern include:

- I will be thinking about you.

- I know this will be difficult.

- You are in my thoughts.

- I loved him/her too.

That's all. You don't necessarily need to elaborate with explanations about how strong I am, how he is in a better place, or how great my future will be. And religious overtones aren't necessary. Think about what you would like to hear if you were highly emotional.

FOLLOW UP WITH CARING GESTURES

It is too difficult for a widow to think, let alone tell someone how they can help. The best thing that someone did for me was to call and say, "I have a frozen chicken pie to deliver to you so that you can have it whenever you like. Would you like for me to drop it off Tuesday or Thursday at 5:00?" I was able to answer that question and appreciated the gift and the five-minute visit.

I couldn't always think to tell someone to do something, like writing down all the food contributions for the funeral. It's okay to take action if you see something that needs to be done.

As time goes by, maybe you could offer to drop off a meal. Ask if you should stay and eat, or if they would like to eat on their own later. That was usually an easier question to answer.

KEEP THE MEMORIES ALIVE

Let's talk about my spouse and some of the things that we remember. If I cry, so what? I appreciate that someone cares enough about him, and me, to talk about the deceased fondly.

Days, weeks, and months down the road, what do you say?

For one thing, you could pick up the phone and call. Just say "I was thinking about you. I know you still miss Gary, and I do too. I always loved it when he talked about your family."

I love it when someone mentions a memory about him. After someone dies, we often act as if that person never existed.

And what if you bump into the person in a grocery store? Say the same kind of thing.

SUPPORT THE NEW LIFESTYLE

Don't tell me I need to mourn more.

Don't tell me I need to date now.

Don't tell me I "should" be over it.

Remember it's not your grief, it is mine to handle as I need to. Everyone is different. If you are lucky, you will not have to experience this in your lifetime.

LISTEN WITH LOVE

No matter what, always listen with love and your efforts will be deeply appreciated.

Hopefully these tips will help you to be more comfortable and confident in providing your best love and support to the widowed.

EPILOGUE – WHERE I AM, REALLY

It is now about five years after Gary's death. I am still on my journey, but life is much brighter. I survived the initial devastation of his death. I am reviving my life, including some aspects of the past, and I'm starting some new things. I am just beginning to thrive and look forward to even better days ahead.

As I already noted, I am seeing light—the beginning of fulfillment of hope and joy in my days. I talk both to my husband and about my husband with a positive attitude. I appreciate personal lessons learned from him and life lessons that we learned together.

Gary is still around me in so many ways. I am comfortable living with his possessions in Marine Corps style, clothes still hanging perfectly on each hanger in his closet and folded neatly in his drawers. I still wear his wedding band. It has not been off my finger since the moment we closed the casket. In fact, it is crowded there with my wedding band, diamond, and another band to hold them all on. I thought that perhaps I would remove them after the first year, but I have felt no reason to. I finally gave away his convertible (that he was planning to trade in) to his favorite charity, Toys for Tots.

His sandals remain by the door in the spot that they have

occupied for years. I still get mail from all the charities that he supported. I have sent money to many of them on his behalf. I will soon be stopping service with the dreaded DECEASED on the return envelope.

But carrying on with things we planned as a couple, initiating personal plans like my traveling and sharing my story through this book are all ways that I am moving along. It keeps the best of our memories and is slowly abandoning the worst of the negativity.

I still have those moments—the ones when I cry and feel hopeless. But they continue to be fewer and further between. I'm sure they will never be completely gone.

Now, though, I can finally say to myself, as well as to the world, how grateful I am for having had the privilege of sharing my life, love, and laughter with Gary M. Drake.

Thanks for the memories.

I love you, Gary, always and forever.

IN MEMORY OF
GARY M. DRAKE

GARY MELVIN DRAKE | 1944 – 2017 | OBITUARY

Funeral Service
Wednesday, Feb 08, 2017

Gary Melvin Drake

March 10, 1944 – February 03, 2017

Gary Melvin Drake, 72, of Arnold Road, Lexington passed away on Friday, February 3, 2017 in Forsyth Medical Center.

A funeral service will be held at 11:00 a.m. Wednesday, February 8, 2017 at Midway United Methodist Church conducted by the Revs. Chuck Ireson, John Woods, and Ray Nance Howell

IV. Burial will follow at Forest Hill Memorial Park Cemetery with Military Honors.

The family will receive friends from 6:00 to 8:00 p.m. Tuesday, February 7, 2017 at Davidson Funeral Home and other times at the home on Arnold Rd.

Mr. Drake was born March 10, 1944 in Watertown, South Dakota, to Melvin Drake and Erma Nelson Drake. He was the Executive Director for the Cancer Services of Davidson County and a member of Midway United Methodist Church. Gary was a veteran having served with the US Marines Corp.

Gary received his BS in History and Political Science from Northern State University in Aberdeen, SD as well as completing graduate hours in Guidance and Counseling. He worked seven years as a high school teacher and coach.

Gary proudly served his country for four years and achieved the rank of Captain in the Marine Corps during the Vietnam era. Then he joined the South Dakota National Guard for eight years and achieved the rank of Major. During this time, he was elected to two terms as South Dakota State Legislator with the distinction at the time of being the youngest representative ever elected.

In South Dakota, much of his career was in radio as General Manager of KCCR/KNEY in Pierre and Advertising Sales Manager of KWAT/KIXX in Watertown. He served as President of Pierre Chamber of Commerce, was a Governor's Appointee to the SD Real Estate Board, and was awarded the Distinguished Service Medal for Meritorious Achievement presented by the Governor and National Guard. Returning to education, he served as Executive Director of the School Administrators of South Dakota. For his many contributions to the state, in 1992 the Governor of South Dakota declared a "Gary Drake Day."

In 1983, he married the love of his life, Sylvia Walters Drake.

They adopted their two children, Michael from Peru and Marisa from Paraguay, and began life in rural North Carolina. As a devoted family man, he always placed top priority on his loving wife Sylvia, his "little princess" daughter Marisa, and his "little Gary" son Michael. As a homeschool dad, he coached basketball, supported Lexington Youth Theatre and provided wonderful real-life and travel experiences. Always active in church, he served on committees and taught Sunday school at Midway United Methodist Church. Most importantly, he served as the best-ever role model for charitable giving and Christian living.

His heart and soul was always devoted to nonprofits and helping people. He worked as CEO of Hospice of Davidson County from 1993 til 2009. He oversaw the dramatic growth expansion of Hospice that included the building of the Hinkle Hospice House. After retiring for three years, he came out of retirement in 2012 to serve as Executive Director of the current Cancer Services of Davidson County working with Ray Nance Howell IV to provide emotional, financial and physical support and information to cancer patients and their families. His greatest days at work were when he was a part of helping make someone's life a little easier in difficult times.

He will be sorely missed by his family and many friends. Semper Fi, until we meet again.

Memorials may be made to Cancer Services of Davidson County, 25 W. 6th Ave., Lexington, NC 27292.

SERVICES

Funeral Service

Wednesday, February 08, 2017
Midway United Methodist Church
9795 Old Hwy 52
Lexington, North Carolina 27295

Davidson Funeral Home, Lexington, NC

Gary Drake Leaves Behind a Legacy of Compassion

February 17, 2017

By Julia Hudgins, The Dispatch, Lexington, NC

Gary Drake's wife, Sylvia Walters Drake, said that in the months prior to his death he repeatedly expressed his contentedness with both his personal and professional life choices.

"I am pretty sure my resume is complete, and I have done what I needed to do," Sylvia recalled her husband saying.

Drake's resume was extensive; before his death on Feb. 3, the 72-year-old devoted nearly 20 years of his life to assisting various local nonprofit organizations. Drake began serving as CEO of Hospice of Davidson County in 1993. The nonprofit flourished under his leadership, stretching to reach more community members and to provide additional services until eventually outgrowing its facilities. From there, Drake oversaw the construction and assisted in the transition of Hospice into the Hinkle Hospice House until retiring in 2009.

However, Drake saw the need at Cancer Services of Davidson County and came out of retirement in 2012 to serve as the nonprofit's executive director. Cancer Services helps community members affected by cancer and their families by providing emotional, financial and physical support and information free of charge to qualified applicants.

Sylvia said compassion was a core aspect of her late husband's personality. It was something she noticed about him immediately, she said, and the trait propelled him forward the 33 years they were married.

"We are extremely proud of everything he did," Sylvia said. "For all the contributions that he made to the community and all the things he did to help others, he was the very same way with (his family)."

'OLD SCHOOL WORK ETHIC'

Ray Nance Howell IV, the current Executive Director of Cancer Services, worked alongside Drake for five years and said that he and Drake were close as colleagues and as friends outside of the office. Howell said he believed Drake thrived during his time at Cancer Services because it married the meticulous and kind portions of his personality.

"I think (Cancer Services) reminded him of the early days of Hospice. ... I think the familial aspect of Cancer Services, and being just a smaller agency, I think (Drake) really enjoyed that because he got to work hand-in-hand with our patients," Howell said. "He got to help people on a daily basis as well as do all of the organizational things that you have to do."

Howell said that Drake had an "old school work ethic" and he seldom missed a day of work. Howell laughed as he recalled how detail-oriented Drake was, and said on the rare occasions he wasn't there he would play good-natured pranks on his longtime coworker.

"On days he wasn't there, on days he had off of work, I would go in and move stuff on his desk, just to mess with him . . ." Howell said with a small smile. "It was always immaculate. If you look at mine it's like a tornado hit it. We were very yin and yang."

In addition to a spotless work space, Howell also remembered how Drake was hardly ever seen without a yellow legal notepad in his hands, ready to jot down ideas and notes. Howell said at Drake's service, they passed around strips of that yellow paper, and those in attendance wrote down personal memories of Drake to give to his family.

LIFE BEFORE DAVIDSON

Prior to his time in Davidson County, Drake lived in South Dakota. There, he served as a captain in the Marine Corps during the Vietnam era; he also served in the South Dakota National Guard for eight years and reached the rank of major. During his time in the National Guard, Drake was one of the youngest representatives ever to be elected to two terms as South Dakota state legislator, and he was awarded the Distinguished Service Medal for Meritorious Achievement presented by the Governor and National Guard.

Drake also served as president of Pierre Chamber of Commerce and was a governor's appointee to the South Dakota Real Estate Board. In 1992, the governor of South Dakota declared a "Gary

Drake Day" as a token of appreciation for his efforts.

Gary received his bachelor's degree in history and political science from Northern State University in Aberdeen, South Dakota. He also completed graduate hours in Guidance and Counseling. He worked seven years as a high school teacher and coach. He also served as Executive Director of the School Administrators of South Dakota.

He worked in radio as General Manager of KCCR/KNEY in Pierre and advertising sales manager of KWAT/KIXX in Watertown while in South Dakota.

'THE BEST KIND OF LOVE'

As she looks back on her husband's full life, Sylvia said she was proud to grow alongside him for 33 years in a relationship she said they both knew would evolve into a cherished marriage by the end of their very first date.

"Gary and I had the best kind of love, we kind of fell in love immediately," Sylvia said.

The couple decided to begin a family, and adopted their son Michael, 25, from Peru, and their daughter, Marisa, 23, from Paraguay. Family life seemed a natural fit for him as he homeschooled his children, coached basketball and supported the Lexington Youth Theatre.

Drake also taught Sunday school at Midway United Methodist Church, where he and his family were active members.

Howell said Drake dedicated his life to the Christian principal of paying it forward to benefit his friends and neighbors. Howell said Drake wanted to "live his faith" and served as a shining example to those around him.

"The idea of helping people in need stemmed from his faith. When Jesus said love your neighbor, Gary took it seriously," Howell said.

His daughter, Marisa, agreed and said she believes he has now moved on to something greater.

"He lived life to its fullest and he completed the task that he set out to do . . ." Marisa said. "He has now moved on to a bigger task."

Though she said she will always feel like there wasn't enough time, Sylvia said she will always treasure the experiences she had with her husband, and that she can see the impact of his strong will and generous nature in not just their family, but in the community he dedicated the latter half of his life to.

"I have just been privileged and honored to have him as my husband and the head of this family for all these years, I think Michael and Marisa have been very blessed to have him as a role model for all the things they needed to learn, believe and do," Sylvia said. "I do feel good that he accomplished the main things he wanted to do. There were other things—there always are—but the big things got done."

Should any community member wish to pay their condolences, the family said in lieu of flowers they request a donation to Cancer Services, the nonprofit that was so close to Drake's heart.

ACKNOWLEDGMENTS

Thank you to my late husband, Gary M. Drake. This book is the direct result of the love and support I had in my life from my husband. It was not just his death, but more importantly, his life that thrust me into a journey of grief and rebuilding, which led to the writing of this book. He inspired me with his mission to help others, and I hope that I am continuing his mission to help others in a way that would please him.

My dear children, Michael and Marisa, lost their daddy way too soon. Although this book does not directly address the loss of a parent, the loss of their daddy is a part of my loss too. I appreciate their support and love them dearly as we continue our family of three here plus one in spirit.

Many thanks to my brother, Perry Walters, who checked on me every day for the first year and most days since to assure that I was surviving. He is my rock.

I am grateful to my dear friend, Jackie Vernon, for being completely available from the first year through today to just listen anytime and respond supportively during my worst moments.

My faithful friend, Debbie Phillips, continues to be a coffee buddy for check-ins every month or two. She has shown deep concern and provided regular feedback on my journey.

Debbie's husband, Mike, and son, Coleman, and other friends helped me around the house and property when I had gotten myself in a bind in the early months. I am so appreciative for all that was done. I needed this support to help get me on track so that I could continue this journey and work on this book.

My deep gratitude goes to my first two friends at Wildacres Fall Gathering who propped up and encouraged me to continue this writing journey. Stacey Donoghue set up the first website and its design. Janie Johnson sketched the first barren widow tree that I continue to use. Other friends at the retreat also cheered me on and inspired me to keep writing in the years after the retreat.

I was encouraged to develop this book by Jones Loflin and Pastor John Woods. They both recognized the need for anything that may be useful for others dealing with a loss such as mine.

My professional colleagues propped me up regularly as I juggled work, grief, and writing. A special thanks goes to Allison Carr, Julie Dixon, and Danielle Richardson.

And a final word of appreciation to my parents, James (Jim) and Louisa Walters, now deceased, for modeling a marriage that was total commitment to each other.

I am indebted to all friends and family whose support has been instrumental in helping me through this journey so that I could complete this book. My intent is to help others to cope with their journey of grief from being widowed.

About the Author

Sylvia A. Walters Drake is living proof that the brokenhearted widowed can survive the devastation of death and move along with life. She has accomplished this by reviving and celebrating the life she and her husband created, and now she is working toward thriving in new ways.

After thirty-three years of marriage to the love of her life, Gary M. Drake, Sylvia is rebuilding a meaningful life. She lives on a small farm in North Carolina with her horse Anastasia, dog Sandie, and cat Midnight. Although she enjoys traveling, trail riding, camping, and daydreaming, her favorite time is spent with family.

Sylvia and Gary adopted their son Michael from Peru and their daughter Marisa from Paraguay. In addition to traveling to those countries, Sylvia has traveled in England, Nepal, India, and about twenty-five other countries. She recently completed a cross-country trip of 11,300 miles, 9 weeks, 24 states, 10 national parks and numerous other public parks, forests, and memorials.

Sylvia is an author, speaker, coach, trainer, entrepreneur, and college professor in communication including self-communication, interpersonal and intercultural communication, and public speaking. She works with individuals, businesses, and associations on national, regional, and local levels.

FREE GIFT
TO HELP YOU ON YOUR JOURNEY...

Download your FREE copy of the Tomorrow Plan to help you begin making small changes tomorrow by starting a little plan today.

Don't wait another moment to get started on creating more direction and purpose as you move along from just surviving toward brighter days ahead.

Get your free downloadable **Tomorrow Plan** here:

www.widowedinaheartbeat.com

THANK YOU FOR READING MY BOOK!

I really appreciate all of your feedback, and I love hearing what you have to say.

I need your input to make the next version of this book and my future books better.

Please leave me an honest review on Amazon with your thoughts on my book.

Thanks so much!

Sylvia A. Walters Drake

To find out more about your Free Gift, the grief journey, additional resources, and future writings, visit www.widowedinaheartbeat.com

www.ingramcontent.com/pod-product-compliance
Lightning Source LLC
Chambersburg PA
CBHW070808280326
41934CB00012B/3110